Mometrix
TEST PREPARATION

Esthetician
Exam Secrets
Study Guide

DEAR FUTURE EXAM SUCCESS STORY

First of all, **THANK YOU** for purchasing Mometrix study materials!

Second, congratulations! You are one of the few determined test-takers who are committed to doing whatever it takes to excel on your exam. **You have come to the right place.** We developed these study materials with one goal in mind: to deliver you the information you need in a format that's concise and easy to use.

In addition to optimizing your guide for the content of the test, we've outlined our recommended steps for breaking down the preparation process into small, attainable goals so you can make sure you stay on track.

We've also analyzed the entire test-taking process, identifying the most common pitfalls and showing how you can overcome them and be ready for any curveball the test throws you.

Standardized testing is one of the biggest obstacles on your road to success, which only increases the importance of doing well in the high-pressure, high-stakes environment of test day. Your results on this test could have a significant impact on your future, and this guide provides the information and practical advice to help you achieve your full potential on test day.

Your success is our success

We would love to hear from you! If you would like to share the story of your exam success or if you have any questions or comments in regard to our products, please contact us at **800-673-8175** or **support@mometrix.com**.

Thanks again for your business and we wish you continued success!

Sincerely,
The Mometrix Test Preparation Team

Need more help? Check out our flashcards at:
http://MometrixFlashcards.com/Esthetician

TABLE OF CONTENTS

Introduction

Thank you for purchasing this resource! You have made the choice to prepare yourself for a test that could have a huge impact on your future, and this guide is designed to help you be fully ready for test day. Obviously, it's important to have a solid understanding of the test material, but you also need to be prepared for the unique environment and stressors of the test, so that you can perform to the best of your abilities.

For this purpose, the first section that appears in this guide is the **Secret Keys**. We've devoted countless hours to meticulously researching what works and what doesn't, and we've boiled down our findings to the five most impactful steps you can take to improve your performance on the test. We start at the beginning with study planning and move through the preparation process, all the way to the testing strategies that will help you get the most out of what you know when you're finally sitting in front of the test.

We recommend that you start preparing for your test as far in advance as possible. However, if you've bought this guide as a last-minute study resource and only have a few days before your test, we recommend that you skip over the first two Secret Keys since they address a long-term study plan.

If you struggle with **test anxiety**, we strongly encourage you to check out our recommendations for how you can overcome it. Test anxiety is a formidable foe, but it can be beaten, and we want to make sure you have the tools you need to defeat it.

Secret Key 1: Plan Big, Study Small

There's a lot riding on your performance. If you want to ace this test, you're going to need to keep your skills sharp and the material fresh in your mind. You need a plan that lets you review everything you need to know while still fitting in your schedule. We'll break this strategy down into three categories.

Information Organization

Start with the information you already have: the official test outline. From this, you can make a complete list of all the concepts you need to cover before the test. Organize these concepts into groups that can be studied together, and create a list of any related vocabulary you need to learn so you can brush up on any difficult terms. You'll want to keep this vocabulary list handy once you actually start studying since you may need to add to it along the way.

Time Management

Once you have your set of study concepts, decide how to spread them out over the time you have left before the test. Break your study plan into small, clear goals so you have a manageable task for each day and know exactly what you're doing. Then just focus on one small step at a time. When you manage your time this way, you don't need to spend hours at a time studying. Studying a small block of content for a short period each day helps you retain information better and avoid stressing over how much you have left to do. You can relax knowing that you have a plan to cover everything in time. In order for this strategy to be effective though, you have to start studying early and stick to your schedule. Avoid the exhaustion and futility that comes from last-minute cramming!

Study Environment

The environment you study in has a big impact on your learning. Studying in a coffee shop, while probably more enjoyable, is not likely to be as fruitful as studying in a quiet room. It's important to keep distractions to a minimum. You're only planning to study for a short block of time, so make the most of it. Don't pause to check your phone or get up to find a snack. It's also important to **avoid multitasking**. Research has consistently shown that multitasking will make your studying dramatically less effective. Your study area should also be comfortable and well-lit so you don't have the distraction of straining your eyes or sitting on an uncomfortable chair.

2

The time of day you study is also important. You want to be rested and alert. Don't wait until just before bedtime. Study when you'll be most likely to comprehend and remember. Even better, if you know what time of day your test will be, set that time aside for study. That way your brain will be used to working on that subject at that specific time and you'll have a better chance of recalling information.

Finally, it can be helpful to team up with others who are studying for the same test. Your actual studying should be done in as isolated an environment as possible, but the work of organizing the information and setting up the study plan can be divided up. In between study sessions, you can discuss with your teammates the concepts that you're all studying and quiz each other on the details. Just be sure that your teammates are as serious about the test as you are. If you find that your study time is being replaced with social time, you might need to find a new team.

Secret Key 2: Make Your Studying Count

You're devoting a lot of time and effort to preparing for this test, so you want to be absolutely certain it will pay off. This means doing more than just reading the content and hoping you can remember it on test day. It's important to make every minute of study count. There are two main areas you can focus on to make your studying count.

Retention

It doesn't matter how much time you study if you can't remember the material. You need to make sure you are retaining the concepts. To check your retention of the information you're learning, try recalling it at later times with minimal prompting. Try carrying around flashcards and glance at one or two from time to time or ask a friend who's also studying for the test to quiz you.

To enhance your retention, look for ways to put the information into practice so that you can apply it rather than simply recalling it. If you're using the information in practical ways, it will be much easier to remember. Similarly, it helps to solidify a concept in your mind if you're not only reading it to yourself but also explaining it to someone else. Ask a friend to let you teach them about a concept you're a little shaky on (or speak aloud to an imaginary audience if necessary). As you try to summarize, define, give examples, and answer your friend's questions, you'll understand the concepts better and they will stay with you longer. Finally, step back for a big picture view and ask yourself how each piece of information fits with the whole subject. When you link the different concepts together and see them working together as a whole, it's easier to remember the individual components.

Finally, practice showing your work on any multi-step problems, even if you're just studying. Writing out each step you take to solve a problem will help solidify the process in your mind, and you'll be more likely to remember it during the test.

Modality

Modality simply refers to the means or method by which you study. Choosing a study modality that fits your own individual learning style is crucial. No two people learn best in exactly the same way, so it's important to know your strengths and use them to your advantage.

4

For example, if you learn best by visualization, focus on visualizing a concept in your mind and draw an image or a diagram. Try color-coding your notes, illustrating them, or creating symbols that will trigger your mind to recall a learned concept. If you learn best by hearing or discussing information, find a study partner who learns the same way or read aloud to yourself. Think about how to put the information in your own words. Imagine that you are giving a lecture on the topic and record yourself so you can listen to it later.

For any learning style, flashcards can be helpful. Organize the information so you can take advantage of spare moments to review. Underline key words or phrases. Use different colors for different categories. Mnemonic devices (such as creating a short list in which every item starts with the same letter) can also help with retention. Find what works best for you and use it to store the information in your mind most effectively and easily.

Secret Key 3: Practice the Right Way

Your success on test day depends not only on how many hours you put into preparing, but also on whether you prepared the right way. It's good to check along the way to see if your studying is paying off. One of the most effective ways to do this is by taking practice tests to evaluate your progress. Practice tests are useful because they show exactly where you need to improve. Every time you take a practice test, pay special attention to these three groups of questions:

- The questions you got wrong
- The questions you had to guess on, even if you guessed right
- The questions you found difficult or slow to work through

This will show you exactly what your weak areas are, and where you need to devote more study time. Ask yourself why each of these questions gave you trouble. Was it because you didn't understand the material? Was it because you didn't remember the vocabulary? Do you need more repetitions on this type of question to build speed and confidence? Dig into those questions and figure out how you can strengthen your weak areas as you go back to review the material.

 Additionally, many practice tests have a section explaining the answer choices. It can be tempting to read the explanation and think that you now have a good understanding of the concept. However, an explanation likely only covers part of the question's broader context. Even if the explanation makes perfect sense, **go back and investigate** every concept related to the question until you're positive you have a thorough understanding.

As you go along, keep in mind that the practice test is just that: practice. Memorizing these questions and answers will not be very helpful on the actual test because it is unlikely to have any of the same exact questions. If you only know the right answers to the sample questions, you won't be prepared for the real thing. **Study the concepts** until you understand them fully, and then you'll be able to answer any question that shows up on the test.

It's important to wait on the practice tests until you're ready. If you take a test on your first day of study, you may be overwhelmed by the amount of material covered and how much you need to learn. Work up to it gradually.

On test day, you'll need to be prepared for answering questions, managing your time, and using the test-taking strategies you've learned. It's a lot to balance, like a mental marathon that will have a big impact on your future. Like training for a marathon, you'll need to start slowly and work your way up. When test day arrives, you'll be ready.

6

Start with the strategies you've read in the first two Secret Keys—plan your course and study in the way that works best for you. If you have time, consider using multiple study resources to get different approaches to the same concepts. It can be helpful to see difficult concepts from more than one angle. Then find a good source for practice tests. Many times, the test website will suggest potential study resources or provide sample tests.

Practice Test Strategy

If you're able to find at least three practice tests, we recommend this strategy:

UNTIMED AND OPEN-BOOK PRACTICE

Take the first test with no time constraints and with your notes and study guide handy. Take your time and focus on applying the strategies you've learned.

TIMED AND OPEN-BOOK PRACTICE

Take the second practice test open-book as well, but set a timer and practice pacing yourself to finish in time.

TIMED AND CLOSED-BOOK PRACTICE

Take any other practice tests as if it were test day. Set a timer and put away your study materials. Sit at a table or desk in a quiet room, imagine yourself at the testing center, and answer questions as quickly and accurately as possible.

Keep repeating timed and closed-book tests on a regular basis until you run out of practice tests or it's time for the actual test. Your mind will be ready for the schedule and stress of test day, and you'll be able to focus on recalling the material you've learned.

Secret Key 4: Pace Yourself

Once you're fully prepared for the material on the test, your biggest challenge on test day will be managing your time. Just knowing that the clock is ticking can make you panic even if you have plenty of time left. Work on pacing yourself so you can build confidence against the time constraints of the exam. Pacing is a difficult skill to master, especially in a high-pressure environment, so **practice is vital**.

Set time expectations for your pace based on how much time is available. For example, if a section has 60 questions and the time limit is 30 minutes, you know you have to average 30 seconds or less per question in order to answer them all. Although 30 seconds is the hard limit, set 25 seconds per question as your goal, so you reserve extra time to spend on harder questions. When you budget extra time for the harder questions, you no longer have any reason to stress when those questions take longer to answer.

Don't let this time expectation distract you from working through the test at a calm, steady pace, but keep it in mind so you don't spend too much time on any one question. Recognize that taking extra time on one question you don't understand may keep you from answering two that you do understand later in the test. If your time limit for a question is up and you're still not sure of the answer, mark it and move on, and come back to it later if the time and the test format allow. If the testing format doesn't allow you to return to earlier questions, just make an educated guess; then put it out of your mind and move on.

On the easier questions, be careful not to rush. It may seem wise to hurry through them so you have more time for the challenging ones, but it's not worth missing one if you know the concept and just didn't take the time to read the question fully. Work efficiently but make sure you understand the question and have looked at all of the answer choices, since more than one may seem right at first.

Even if you're paying attention to the time, you may find yourself a little behind at some point. You should speed up to get back on track, but do so wisely. Don't panic; just take a few seconds less on each question until you're caught up. Don't guess without thinking, but do look through the answer choices and eliminate any you know are wrong. If you can get down to two choices, it is often worthwhile to guess from those. Once you've chosen an answer, move on and don't dwell on any that you skipped or had to hurry through. If a question was taking too long, chances are it was one of the harder ones, so you weren't as likely to get it right anyway.

On the other hand, if you find yourself getting ahead of schedule, it may be beneficial to slow down a little. The more quickly you work, the more likely you are to make a careless mistake that will affect your score. You've budgeted time for each question, so don't be afraid to spend that time. Practice an efficient but careful pace to get the most out of the time you have.

Secret Key 5: Have a Plan for Guessing

When you're taking the test, you may find yourself stuck on a question. Some of the answer choices seem better than others, but you don't see the one answer choice that is obviously correct. What do you do?

The scenario described above is very common, yet most test takers have not effectively prepared for it. Developing and practicing a plan for guessing may be one of the single most effective uses of your time as you get ready for the exam.

In developing your plan for guessing, there are three questions to address:

- When should you start the guessing process?
- How should you narrow down the choices?
- Which answer should you choose?

When to Start the Guessing Process

Unless your plan for guessing is to select C every time (which, despite its merits, is not what we recommend), you need to leave yourself enough time to apply your answer elimination strategies. Since you have a limited amount of time for each question, that means that if you're going to give yourself the best shot at guessing correctly, you have to decide quickly whether or not you will guess.

Of course, the best-case scenario is that you don't have to guess at all, so first, see if you can answer the question based on your knowledge of the subject and basic reasoning skills. Focus on the key words in the question and try to jog your memory of related topics. Give yourself a chance to bring the knowledge to mind, but once you realize that you don't have (or you can't access) the knowledge you need to answer the question, it's time to start the guessing process.

It's almost always better to start the guessing process too early than too late. It only takes a few seconds to remember something and answer the question from knowledge. Carefully eliminating wrong answer choices takes longer. Plus, going through the process of eliminating answer choices can actually help jog your memory.

Summary: Start the guessing process as soon as you decide that you can't answer the question based on your knowledge.

How to Narrow Down the Choices

The next chapter in this book (**Test-Taking Strategies**) includes a wide range of strategies for how to approach questions and how to look for answer choices to eliminate. You will definitely want to read those carefully, practice them, and figure out which ones work best for you. Here though, we're going to address a mindset rather than a particular strategy.

Your odds of guessing an answer correctly depend on how many options you are choosing from.

Number of options left	5	4	3	2	1
Odds of guessing correctly	20%	25%	33%	50%	100%

You can see from this chart just how valuable it is to be able to eliminate incorrect answers and make an educated guess, but there are two things that many test takers do that cause them to miss out on the benefits of guessing:

- Accidentally eliminating the correct answer
- Selecting an answer based on an impression

We'll look at the first one here, and the second one in the next section.

To avoid accidentally eliminating the correct answer, we recommend a thought exercise called **the $5 challenge**. In this challenge, you only eliminate an answer choice from contention if you are willing to bet $5 on it being wrong. Why $5? Five dollars is a small but not insignificant amount of money. It's an amount you could

afford to lose but wouldn't want to throw away. And while losing $5 once might not hurt too much, doing it twenty times will set you back $100. In the same way, each small decision you make—eliminating a choice here, guessing on a question there—won't by itself impact your score very much, but when you put them all together, they can make a big difference. By holding each answer choice elimination decision to a higher standard, you can reduce the risk of accidentally eliminating the correct answer.

The $5 challenge can also be applied in a positive sense: If you are willing to bet $5 that an answer choice *is* correct, go ahead and mark it as correct.

Summary: Only eliminate an answer choice if you are willing to bet $5 that it is wrong.

11

Which Answer to Choose

You're taking the test. You've run into a hard question and decided you'll have to guess. You've eliminated all the answer choices you're willing to bet $5 on. Now you have to pick an answer. Why do we even need to talk about this? Why can't you just pick whichever one you feel like when the time comes?

The answer to these questions is that if you don't come into the test with a plan, you'll rely on your impression to select an answer choice, and if you do that, you risk falling into a trap. The test writers know that everyone who takes their test will be guessing on some of the questions, so they intentionally write wrong answer choices to seem plausible. You still have to pick an answer though, and if the wrong answer choices are designed to look right, how can you ever be sure that you're not falling for their trap? The best solution we've found to this dilemma is to take the decision out of your hands entirely. Here is the process we recommend:

Once you've eliminated any choices that you are confident (willing to bet $5) are wrong, select the first remaining choice as your answer.

Whether you choose to select the first remaining choice, the second, or the last, the important thing is that you use some preselected standard. Using this approach guarantees that you will not be enticed into selecting an answer choice that looks right, because you are not basing your decision on how the answer choices look.

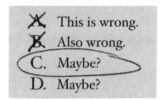

This is not meant to make you question your knowledge. Instead, it is to help you recognize the difference between your knowledge and your impressions. There's a huge difference between thinking an answer is right because of what you know, and thinking an answer is right because it looks or sounds like it should be right.

Summary: To ensure that your selection is appropriately random, make a predetermined selection from among all answer choices you have not eliminated.

12

Test-Taking Strategies

This section contains a list of test-taking strategies that you may find helpful as you work through the test. By taking what you know and applying logical thought, you can maximize your chances of answering any question correctly!

It is very important to realize that every question is different and every person is different: no single strategy will work on every question, and no single strategy will work for every person. That's why we've included all of them here, so you can try them out and determine which ones work best for different types of questions and which ones work best for you.

Question Strategies

⊘ READ CAREFULLY

Read the question and the answer choices carefully. Don't miss the question because you misread the terms. You have plenty of time to read each question thoroughly and make sure you understand what is being asked. Yet a happy medium must be attained, so don't waste too much time. You must read carefully and efficiently.

⊘ CONTEXTUAL CLUES

Look for contextual clues. If the question includes a word you are not familiar with, look at the immediate context for some indication of what the word might mean. Contextual clues can often give you all the information you need to decipher the meaning of an unfamiliar word. Even if you can't determine the meaning, you may be able to narrow down the possibilities enough to make a solid guess at the answer to the question.

⊘ PREFIXES

If you're having trouble with a word in the question or answer choices, try dissecting it. Take advantage of every clue that the word might include. Prefixes can be a huge help. Usually, they allow you to determine a basic meaning. *Pre-* means before, *post-* means after, *pro-* is positive, *de-* is negative. From prefixes, you can get an idea of the general meaning of the word and try to put it into context.

⊘ HEDGE WORDS

Watch out for critical hedge words, such as *likely, may, can, sometimes, often, almost, mostly, usually, generally, rarely,* and *sometimes.* Question writers insert these hedge phrases to cover every possibility. Often an answer choice will be wrong simply because it leaves no room for exception. Be on guard for answer choices that have definitive words such as *exactly* and *always.*

13

⊘ Switchback Words

Stay alert for *switchbacks*. These are the words and phrases frequently used to alert you to shifts in thought. The most common switchback words are *but, although*, and *however*. Others include *nevertheless, on the other hand, even though, while, in spite of, despite*, and *regardless of.* Switchback words are important to catch because they can change the direction of the question or an answer choice.

⊘ Face Value

When in doubt, use common sense. Accept the situation in the problem at face value. Don't read too much into it. These problems will not require you to make wild assumptions. If you have to go beyond creativity and warp time or space in order to have an answer choice fit the question, then you should move on and consider the other answer choices. These are normal problems rooted in reality. The applicable relationship or explanation may not be readily apparent, but it is there for you to figure out. Use your common sense to interpret anything that isn't clear.

Answer Choice Strategies

⊘ Answer Selection

The most thorough way to pick an answer choice is to identify and eliminate wrong answers until only one is left, then confirm it is the correct answer. Sometimes an answer choice may immediately seem right, but be careful. The test writers will usually put more than one reasonable answer choice on each question, so take a second to read all of them and make sure that the other choices are not equally obvious. As long as you have time left, it is better to read every answer choice than to pick the first one that looks right without checking the others.

⊘ Answer Choice Families

An answer choice family consists of two (in rare cases, three) answer choices that are very similar in construction and cannot all be true at the same time. If you see two answer choices that are direct opposites or parallels, one of them is usually the correct answer. For instance, if one answer choice says that quantity x increases and another either says that quantity x decreases (opposite) or says that quantity y increases (parallel), then those answer choices would fall into the same family. An answer choice that doesn't match the construction of the answer choice family is more likely to be incorrect. Most questions will not have answer choice families, but when they do appear, you should be prepared to recognize them.

⊘ Eliminate Answers

Eliminate answer choices as soon as you realize they are wrong, but make sure you consider all possibilities. If you are eliminating answer choices and realize that the last one you are left with is also wrong, don't panic. Start over and consider each choice again. There may be something you missed the first time that you will realize on the second pass.

⊘ Avoid Fact Traps

Don't be distracted by an answer choice that is factually true but doesn't answer the question. You are looking for the choice that answers the question. Stay focused on what the question is asking for so you don't accidentally pick an answer that is true but incorrect. Always go back to the question and make sure the answer choice you've selected actually answers the question and is not merely a true statement.

⊘ Extreme Statements

In general, you should avoid answers that put forth extreme actions as standard practice or proclaim controversial ideas as established fact. An answer choice that states the "process should be used in certain situations, if..." is much more likely to be correct than one that states the "process should be discontinued completely." The first is a calm rational statement and doesn't even make a definitive, uncompromising stance, using a hedge word *if* to provide wiggle room, whereas the second choice is far more extreme.

⊘ Benchmark

As you read through the answer choices and you come across one that seems to answer the question well, mentally select that answer choice. This is not your final answer, but it's the one that will help you evaluate the other answer choices. The one that you selected is your benchmark or standard for judging each of the other answer choices. Every other answer choice must be compared to your benchmark. That choice is correct until proven otherwise by another answer choice beating it. If you find a better answer, then that one becomes your new benchmark. Once you've decided that no other choice answers the question as well as your benchmark, you have your final answer.

⊘ Predict the Answer

Before you even start looking at the answer choices, it is often best to try to predict the answer. When you come up with the answer on your own, it is easier to avoid distractions and traps because you will know exactly what to look for. The right answer choice is unlikely to be word-for-word what you came up with, but it should be a close match. Even if you are confident that you have the right answer, you should still take the time to read each option before moving on.

General Strategies

⊘ Tough Questions

If you are stumped on a problem or it appears too hard or too difficult, don't waste time. Move on! Remember though, if you can quickly check for obviously incorrect answer choices, your chances of guessing correctly are greatly improved. Before you completely give up, at least try to knock out a couple of possible answers. Eliminate what you can and then guess at the remaining answer choices before moving on.

15

⊘ Check Your Work

Since you will probably not know every term listed and the answer to every question, it is important that you get credit for the ones that you do know. Don't miss any questions through careless mistakes. If at all possible, try to take a second to look back over your answer selection and make sure you've selected the correct answer choice and haven't made a costly careless mistake (such as marking an answer choice that you didn't mean to mark). This quick double check should more than pay for itself in caught mistakes for the time it costs.

⊘ Pace Yourself

It's easy to be overwhelmed when you're looking at a page full of questions; your mind is confused and full of random thoughts, and the clock is ticking down faster than you would like. Calm down and maintain the pace that you have set for yourself. Especially as you get down to the last few minutes of the test, don't let the small numbers on the clock make you panic. As long as you are on track by monitoring your pace, you are guaranteed to have time for each question.

⊘ Don't Rush

It is very easy to make errors when you are in a hurry. Maintaining a fast pace in answering questions is pointless if it makes you miss questions that you would have gotten right otherwise. Test writers like to include distracting information and wrong answers that seem right. Taking a little extra time to avoid careless mistakes can make all the difference in your test score. Find a pace that allows you to be confident in the answers that you select.

⊘ Keep Moving

Panicking will not help you pass the test, so do your best to stay calm and keep moving. Taking deep breaths and going through the answer elimination steps you practiced can help to break through a stress barrier and keep your pace.

Final Notes

The combination of a solid foundation of content knowledge and the confidence that comes from practicing your plan for applying that knowledge is the key to maximizing your performance on test day. As your foundation of content knowledge is built up and strengthened, you'll find that the strategies included in this chapter become more and more effective in helping you quickly sift through the distractions and traps of the test to isolate the correct answer.

Now that you're preparing to move forward into the test content chapters of this book, be sure to keep your goal in mind. As you read, think about how you will be able to apply this information on the test. If you've already seen sample questions for the test and you have an idea of the question format and style, try to come up with questions of your own that you can answer based on what you're reading. This will give you valuable practice applying your knowledge in the same ways you can expect to on test day.

Good luck and good studying!

Scientific Concepts

Basic Microbiology

Bacteria are a group of single celled microorganisms that can be categorized as pathogenic or nonpathogenic. Pathogenic bacteria spread disease and infection and need to be carefully eliminated to maintain a safe, healthy environment. Nonpathogenic bacteria do not carry the risk of disease and are necessary for some bodily functions.

Pathogenic bacteria are responsible for the spread of bacterial infections. Infections from these bacteria are characterized by the presence of inflammation and/or pus. These infections may be localized to one area on the body and appear as an abscess or lesion, or they may spread throughout the body, resulting in systemic infection. Staphylococcus is a common family of bacteria that are typically harmless. However, some strains cause strep throat, food poisoning, and flesh-eating disease. Methicillin-resistant staphylococcus aureus (MRSA) is a strain resistant to treatment that can be contracted from contaminated items during beauty treatments. Therefore, adherence to proper infection control protocols and refusal of services to clients presenting signs of infection are critical. Mycobacterium, a family of bacteria found in soil or water, has been linked to infections following pedicures. Therefore, disinfection of all tools and basins that contact water and refusal of service to clients with damaged or broken skin are important infection control procedures.

Viruses are microorganisms that infect cells and can cause disease. Viruses require hosts to replicate and spread. Viruses can cause a range of diseases including the common cold, HIV, and were even the source of some historical plague events. Viruses cannot be cured. However, many viruses such as measles and chickenpox can be prevented through use of vaccines. For viruses for which vaccines have not been developed, spread can be prevented through regular handwashing and disinfecting. Some viruses, such as Human papilloma virus and Herpes simplex virus, can be spread through direct and indirect contact. Other viruses, such as hepatitis and HIV, are bloodborne pathogens that spread from specific bodily fluids through orifices or broken skin. Symptoms may not be evident for several days following viral infection, and some viruses do not cause outward symptoms. However, the absence of symptoms does not indicate whether an individual is contagious. Therefore, prevention methods must be implemented for clients, as infection status may not be apparent.

Fungi are spore-producing organisms such as molds, mushrooms, and yeast. The most commonly occurring fungal infections following esthetic services are tinea barbae, which causes inflamed skin on the face and neck, and tinea capitis, which causes inflammation around hair follicles. Each of these typically occur as a result of unsanitary tool usage during a haircut.

19

Parasites are organisms that live on or within a host. In beauty services head lice are a common parasite. Scabies, which are small parasitic mites that burrow into skin, are also common. These mites are not readily visible, but the resultant lesions can be easily identified. Refusing services to clients with visible parasitic infestations is a preventive barrier to minimize parasite transmission. Disinfection is a secondary, yet essential preventive barrier, as it is possible that parasites and their indicators are not yet visible on a client.

Biofilms are colonies of microorganisms that grow and cement together to create a solid and unpliable structure. In the beauty industry, biofilms are likely to grow in foot spas and in sinks. If they enter the body, they can grow and cause illnesses that are antibiotic resistant, as biofilms prevent antibiotics from reaching the infection. Biofilms are hard to detect and have not been extensively studied. Therefore, standard infection control procedures are critical to prevention of biofilm formation.

Infection Control Procedures

Infection control refers to processes implemented to eliminate or reduce the risk of spread of communicable illness, bacteria, or infectious disease. For esthetic professionals this means maintaining a sanitary workspace with properly treated tools and equipment and following the guidelines established by both federal and state agencies. These guidelines and procedures include proper handwashing, use of sanitation equipment and disinfecting solutions, and regular cleaning of the work environment. Failure to adhere to safe work practices and infection control guidelines can lead to spread of infectious organisms between clients and to the esthetic professional. Serious injury, illness, and death can occur if proper infection control practices are not followed. Therefore, understanding and following these practices is crucial in the esthetics industry.

Infection control consists of four tiers of elimination of infectious organisms: cleaning, sanitizing, disinfecting, and sterilizing. These tiers may be used in combination, but each term has its own specific meaning and function. Cleaning refers to removal of visible debris and some infectious organisms using soap or a cleansing detergent and water. Cleaning is the most basic level of infection control but does not eliminate all infectious organisms on its own. Therefore, cleaning precedes the other infection control methods. Sanitizing reduces infectious organisms on the surface through use of chemicals. Disinfecting also uses chemicals, but differs from sanitizing in that it destroys infectious organisms in addition to reducing the number present. Sterilizing is the most intense method of infection control because it destroys all infectious organisms. Sterilization is typically accomplished using an autoclave that uses steam to sterilize tools and implements.

Infection transmission refers to the way in which pathogens move. Direct transmission is the transfer of pathogens directly from one person to another through contact such as touching, sneezing, or coughing. Direct transmission is the primary mode of transmission for viruses, parasitic infections, and warts. The risk of contracting an illness through direct transmission is decreased through regular handwashing. Indirect transmission occurs through contact with a contaminated surface or object, such as a contaminated implement. Salmonella, ringworm, and MRSA are transmitted through indirect transmission. Use of proper infection control methods reduces the risk of indirect transmission by eliminating pathogens on tools and surfaces. Airborne transmission occurs when pathogens expressed through talking, coughing, or sneezing are suspended in the air, then inhaled by another individual. A number of illnesses including the common cold and measles can spread through airborne transmission. Wearing a mask when sick and for a number of days following illness helps prevent airborne transmission.

Infection prevention is typically viewed as a two-step process consisting of cleaning and disinfecting. Cleaning is the process of removing all visible dirt and debris with water and some form of soap, detergent, or chemical cleaner using a brush or sponge. Once all debris, oil, and residue are removed, the tool or surface is ready for disinfection. Failing to remove the debris, oil, or residue may prevent the disinfectant from reaching the surface, thus reducing its ability to eliminate infectious pathogens.

Cleaning hands is as important as cleaning surfaces. Handwashing is the first step in preventing the spread of disease. The friction from handwashing pulls pathogens from the surface of the hand. A provider's hands should be washed immediately before and after services. When handwashing is not a viable or practical option, use of waterless hand sanitizers is acceptable. Hand sanitizers include antiseptics, such as alcohol, as ingredients to kill germs on the skin.

Disinfecting is the second step in the two-step infection prevention process. Disinfection eliminates most of the microorganisms on a surface through use of a disinfectant. Disinfectants destroy bacteria, fungi, and viruses on inanimate surfaces and are not to be used directly on clients. The first step in disinfection is selecting and preparing the proper disinfectant. Disinfectants vary in mixing ratios, which indicates the amount of water to be mixed with the concentrated solution, and contact time, which is the amount of time the disinfecting solution must remain in contact with the surface to effectively kill pathogens. Some disinfectants come fully prepared to use. Because of variability among disinfectants, all instructions should be read carefully before use. Disinfectant concentrates are caustic and corrosive chemicals. Therefore, safety equipment should be worn while mixing it. Once a disinfectant is ready for use, the surface or tool being disinfected should be cleaned to ensure the disinfectant can work effectively and reach all pathogens. It is necessary to adhere to all manufacturer guidelines to ensure proper use.

The three most commonly used disinfectants in the beauty industry are quats, tuberculocidal disinfectants, and bleach.

Quats is shorthand for quaternary ammonium compounds. These disinfectants are highly effective on nonporous surfaces and tools. Some disinfectants contain a blend of quats to increase efficacy.

Tuberculocidal disinfectants are designed to kill tuberculosis bacteria and many other pathogens. Use of these disinfectants is required in some cases. However, these disinfectants can be extremely harmful to humans and the environment if used improperly. Therefore, these disinfectants should only be used when required by state regulations.

Chlorine bleach is an effective disinfectant commonly used in the beauty industry. It must be diluted with water according to manufacturer directions and used within 24 hours to be effective. Only bleach products registered with the EPA are considered disinfectants. Therefore, it is necessary to check the label before using bleach to disinfect. Bleach is most commonly used as a surface cleaner.

Nonporous items and surfaces, defined as those without liquid absorbing pores, are common breeding grounds for bacteria and can promote infection through indirect transmission. Therefore, these surfaces must be cleaned and disinfected between uses. Items with no electrical components, such as brushes, combs, and shears, should be disinfected according to the manufacturer's instructions. In most cases these items will be submerged in a disinfecting solution made from concentrated disinfectant and water. Items that have electrical contact points, such as clippers, cannot be submerged in a disinfecting solution and require special care. They should be cleaned with an EPA registered disinfectant specifically made for these tools following the tool manufacturer's instructions. Disinfected work surfaces such as tables, chairs, and sinks require extended surface contact with the disinfectant according to the manufacturer's instructions prior to being wiped down. Proper disinfecting practices help prevent the spread of pathogens among clients.

Porous items are those that absorb liquid through holes in their surface. These items require laundering to be cleaned and sanitized. In a salon setting these items include capes, towels, and linens. These items should be laundered according to the manufacturer's instructions. Once washed, they should be dried thoroughly to prevent any mildew or bacterial growth. Soiled linens and towels should be kept covered or contained and stored away from clean linens to prevent cross contamination. When possible, it is recommended to use single use, disposable items. When single use items are not an option, these items should be cleaned prior to use on each client.

Many products found in salon settings are multiuse, including hair products and moisturizing treatments. There is no way to disinfect or sanitize these items, therefore they must be kept sanitary throughout their lifespan. Pump dispensers or shakers should be used to dispense bottle products, and products in a tub should be dispensed using a clean spatula or scoop. This prevents pathogens from entering into and growing in the product. Contaminated products should be disposed of immediately.

Sterilization is a process that destroys all microbial life on a surface. Sterilization is not required in most salon settings as only reusable implements that will be entering the body must be sterilized between uses. However, sterilization can be used as an extreme method of infection control if desired. Sterilization is most often completed using an autoclave. Autoclaves are machines that use heat and pressure to destroy any organisms, including spores, living on the surfaces of items. The Center for Disease Control and Prevention (CDC) mandates that autoclaves be tested monthly to ensure efficacy. The high cost and burdensome maintenance schedules associated with autoclaves preclude most salons from using sterilization as an infection control procedure.

Safety Procedures and Guidelines

Federal agencies are entities established by the federal government that are responsible for regulation of equipment and chemicals in the workplace. Furthermore, federal agencies monitor workplace safety and services offered. The Occupational Safety and Health Administration (OSHA) plays a significant role in the beauty industry due to frequent product use. OSHA requires manufacturers to provide Safety Data Sheets that provide instructions for safe use and disposal of all potentially hazardous materials. The Environmental Protection Agency (EPA) regulates all disinfectants used in the US. As disinfection is a key component of infection control in the beauty industry, EPA guidelines must be followed to prevent breaking the law.

State agencies regulate licensure and enforce health and safety guidelines through inspection and investigation of complaints. Regulations and requirements vary by state, which requires each esthetician to be familiar with applicable state rules. These agencies include licensing agencies, health departments, and state boards.

For services where water will be applied directly to a client's body, such as shampooing or rinsing hair, maintenance of appropriate water temperature is critical. Water that is too hot can cause serious injury. Injury can be prevented by testing the temperature of the water before beginning the service and by turning the thermostat on the hot water heater down to an acceptable level. This will prevent the water from ever reaching dangerous temperatures. The water should still be tested before beginning services even when the thermostat has been adjusted. In addition, the temperature of any steam or hot towel services should be tested to prevent burns. This testing is completed by applying the water or towel to the inside of the provider's wrist to determine if the temperature is appropriate. For steam treatments, the provider should place their wrist over the steam to test the temperature before allowing the client access.

Water on the floor creates a fall risk for clients and providers. This can be prevented by carefully handling the spray hose during services. Any spilled water should be cleaned immediately, and wet floor signs should be placed to inform others of the risk.

Most accidents and injuries in salon and spa settings can be avoided by reducing safety hazard risks. Developing a well-planned workstation is key to maintaining safe access to tools and appliances. By planning a station around electrical outlets, providers minimize the risk of tripping over cords or having cords wrapped around their furniture. Storing disinfecting jars where they are not likely to be accidentally bumped or spilled prevents glass breakage and chemical spill hazards. Appropriate tool storage, such as containing smaller tools and mounting large equipment, provides easy access to tools while preventing hazard scenarios. If a provider notices damage to a tool or equipment, they should immediately stop using it until it is repaired or replaced. Repairs should only be performed by the manufacturer of the tool, not the provider, to ensure safety. Fixtures such as chairs, tables, and lamps should be kept clean to maintain a safe working environment.

Due to frequent use of chemicals and products in salons and spas, proper ventilation is crucial to protect the respiratory health of clients and providers. Overexposure to chemical fumes and particles from products can cause allergies, respiratory issues, and other related health problems. Cleaning vents prevent buildup of hair, dust, and products that may impede proper ventilation, and allow for air to circulate thoroughly. It may be necessary to install filtration systems to help keep the air clean. This is especially true in areas where chemical and nail treatments are performed, as these require specific air filtration to remove fumes and particles from the air. These systems must be maintained and cleaned regularly to ensure they work appropriately. Exits should be marked and kept clear so they are easy to access in the event of an emergency. The same applies to fire extinguishers. Extinguishers should be inspected periodically, and all employees should be trained in their use.

Because children can cause risk to themselves, service providers, and salon environments, they should not be left unattended. Patrons should be advised of the potential risks and reminded frequently of these risks to help ensure the safety of their children. When providing services, the provider should try to anticipate the child's actions and movements and gently but firmly help the child maintain an appropriate posture with one hand while working with the other.

Adult clients do not typically require the same amount of guidance or assistance as children; however, older clients may need help getting into and out of chairs where services are provided. Assistance should be offered to all clients, as the need for help is not always visible and physical capabilities should not be assumed. Adult clients should be informed of the risks of services they are receiving so they can make informed decisions.

High-risk clients are those with preexisting medical conditions that may inhibit their immune systems. While it is necessary to use clean, disinfected tools with all clients, providers should take extra care with high-risk clients.

Service providers are responsible for being familiar with and following local and federal law regarding health and safety. This protects both the clients and the provider from illnesses and injuries. Providers must also stay abreast of changes to state rules and regulations and are responsible for maintaining their license with state agencies.

Emergency preparedness ensures safety by preparing employees for potential life-threatening situations. Maintaining emergency information for all employees and clients, such as family contacts and medical conditions, will aid first responders in the event of a medical emergency. Employees should be well versed in fire safety, poison control procedures, basic first aid, and how to contact medical rescue in the event of an emergency.

Having easy access to contact information for utility and custodial services can be useful in the event of an emergency or issue in the salon or shop. Therefore, this information should be reviewed often and kept current. Maintaining a clean, organized, and safe workspace allows providers to take pride in their services and client care.

STANDARD (UNIVERSAL) PRECAUTIONS

Standard Precautions are guidelines developed and published by the Center for Disease Control and Prevention (CDC) that require professionals providing treatments where bodily fluids are or may be, present as if those fluids are carrying an infectious disease. Because some clients may not display symptoms of communicable disease or infection while they are contagious, this helps prevent spread by ensuring infection control practices are used for all clients. Standard Precautions requires use of personal protective equipment (PPE), such as gloves and masks, to protect individuals from contracting and transmitting pathogens. Gloves are considered single use PPE and should be disposed of between clients and changed anytime during a service when they may have become contaminated. It is also necessary for the provider to wash their hands after removing and before putting on a pair of gloves. Standard Precautions also outlines the required procedure for disposing of any instrument that has come in contact with blood or other bodily fluids. Following Standard Precautions helps to keep all clients and salon staff free from infectious diseases.

BLOOD EXPOSURE PROCEDURES

An exposure incident is any contact made with broken skin through which contact with blood or bodily fluid may occur. In adherence with CDC Standard Precautions, it is necessary to act as though all clients may carry pathogens that can lead to infection. If a client suffers a cut or abrasion during services, the provider should immediately stop services, put on gloves if they are not already wearing them, and apologize for the incident. The client should wash and dry the injured area. The provider should offer antiseptic and bandages for the injured area. Once the client has been cared for, the provider should clean and disinfect their workstation in adherence with Standard Precautions and local law for disposal of contaminants. Contaminated gloves should be disposed of. The provider should then wash their hands and put on clean gloves before cleaning and disinfecting tools and implements used during the service. The provider should once again dispose of their gloves and wash their hands before offering to continue services if appropriate. The same procedure should be followed if the injury occurs to the service provider.

HANDLING OF CHEMICALS

A variety of chemicals are used in beauty service, and improper use can lead to injury, illness, and even death in some cases. Thoroughly reading labels will prevent misuse in many cases. Labels must adhere to EPA or FDA requirements and disclose all potential hazards. Other considerations include:

- **Transportation**: All chemicals should be transported in their original, unopened containers. This prevents spilling or mixing of fumes. Some chemicals should not be exposed to heat or direct light, so transporting them in a vehicle on warm days without taking precautions can lead to dangerous chemical reactions.
- **Storage**: All chemicals should be stored in their original containers to prevent potential confusion over what is actually in a container and because some chemicals can have dangerous reactions when combined. For example, acetone and hydrogen peroxide can form volatile and explosive peroxides if mixed together. It is also particularly important to store chemicals out of reach of children.
- **Mixing**: As mentioned previously, mixing chemicals can lead to negative consequences. It is important to ensure that the chemicals being mixed are compatible. When mixing, providers should use personal protective equipment, such as gloves, and work in a well-ventilated area.
- **Disposal**: Not all chemicals can be disposed of down a drain due to their potential environmental impact. As such, providers need to familiarize themselves with proper disposal techniques, such as chemical waste recycling.

Safety Data Sheets are legally required to accompany chemicals to be used in the workplace. They provide the information needed to safely use, store, and dispose of chemicals. They contain the following 16 categories:

- **Identification**: Name of product and manufacturer/distributor
- **Hazard Identification**: List of all associated hazards
- **Composition/Information on Ingredients**: List of all ingredients
- **First-Aid Measures**: Symptoms of exposure and treatment
- **Fire-Fighting Methods**: How to safely extinguish
- **Accidental Release Measures**: Proper cleanup of spills
- **Handling and Storage**: Safe handling and storing instructions
- **Exposure Control/Personal Protection**: Limits on exposure
- **Physical and Chemical Properties**: List of all properties of the chemical
- **Stability and Reactivity**: Environmental stability and reaction
- **Toxicological Information**: Measure of toxicity and overexposure symptoms
- **Ecological Information**: Danger to the environment
- **Disposal Considerations**: How to dispose of the chemical
- **Transportation Information**: Guidelines and restrictions for transport

26

- **Regulatory Information**: Any specific related regulations
- **Other Information**: When the SDS was created or last revised

Human Physiology and Anatomy

CELLS AND THEIR FUNCTIONS

Cells are the basic unit of life that make up all living organisms. There are a variety of cells in the human body, and they are all composed of **protoplasm**, a colorless, gel-like substance that contains the nutrients for the cell. Organelles are specialized structures within cells that are also contained within the protoplasm. The **nucleus** is an organelle at the center of the cell that contains a fluid called **nucleoplasm** that houses **deoxyribonucleic acid** (DNA). DNA determines a living organism's genetic makeup. **Mitochondria** are organelles often referred to as "the powerhouse of the cell." They create energy through uptake and breakdown of nutrients to create chemical energy in the form of **adenosine triphosphate** (ATP). The **cell membrane** encloses the protoplasm and acts as the outside of the cell. It is permeable and allows nutrients to enter the cell and allows waste to be removed.

Mitosis is the process of cell reproduction in human tissue. Chromosomes in the cell are replicated, then split to form two identical cells with their own nuclei. These are called **daughter cells**. The daughter cells then grow and undergo mitosis. The process continues as long as conditions are favorable for cell growth. Cells require nutrients, oxygen, water, and suitable temperatures to reproduce. They must also be able to eliminate waste products. If favorable conditions do not exist or are not adequate, cells will fail to reproduce. Cell reproduction will also not occur in the presence of toxins, diseases, or injury as these conditions can cause cell damage or death. Mitosis occurs continuously throughout the human body with most cells taking about 24 hours to complete the cycle.

Metabolism in cells is a set of biochemical processes responsible for converting nutrients to energy and for eliminating waste products from the cell, allowing cells to continue to grow and reproduce. As humans age, their cell metabolism slows, impacting the skin's response time to active ingredients used in skincare. Slower cell metabolism results in slower reaction to skincare products. Slower metabolism also leads to an increase in visible signs of aging in the skin such as fine lines and wrinkles. This requires aging skin to be treated with products that boost metabolism and reduce the appearance of wrinkles. Exfoliating helps to remove cells that are dead or reproducing slowly. Products containing antioxidants protect the cells from free radicals that slow healing. Consumption of water for hydration helps boost cell metabolism by creating an environment ideal for cell reproduction.

TISSUES

Tissue is a group of cells that performs a specific function. There are four types of tissues in the human body:

- **Connective**: Connective tissue supports or binds other tissues of the body together. Examples of connective tissue include bones, cartilage, fat, and blood. Esthetics-related examples include collagen and elastin.
- **Epithelial**: Epithelial tissue forms the protective lining of body cavities and organ surfaces. Skin, mucous membranes, glands, and the linings of the digestive system, heart, and respiratory organs are examples.
- **Muscle**: Muscle tissue moves parts of the body by contracting. Nearly all movement of the body requires use of muscle tissue, including internal movements such as swallowing, urinating, or digesting food.
- **Nerve**: Nerve tissue is composed of specialized cells called neurons that carry messages throughout the nervous system. The brain and the spinal cord contain nerve tissue.

ORGANS AND THEIR FUNCTION

Organs are a collection of tissues that form a structure that performs a specific task within the body. Examples include the heart, lungs, brain, and stomach. **Body systems** are groups of organs that work together to produce specific body functions. Knowing the body systems and their functions will assist an esthetician in making informed decisions during treatments. For example, understanding the muscular system allows for safe and effective massage. The body systems and the organs they consist of are:

- **Integumentary system**: Skin, oil and sweat glands, sensory receptors, hair, and nails
- **Skeletal system**: Bones
- **Muscular system**: Muscle
- **Nervous system**: Brain, spinal cord, and nerves
- **Circulatory system**: Heart and blood vessels
- **Immune/lymphatic system**: Spleen, bone marrow, and thymus
- **Endocrine system**: Adrenal glands
- **Reproductive system**: Uterus and ovaries for females, penis and testes for males
- **Respiratory system**: Lungs, trachea, and bronchi
- **Digestive system**: Esophagus, stomach, gallbladder, liver, small and large intestines
- **Excretory system**: Kidneys and bladder

SYSTEMS AND THEIR FUNCTIONS

The bones of the skull are divided into cranial bones and facial bones. The **cranium** is the portion of the skull that protects the brain and comprises eight bones:

Bone	Location
Occipital Bone	Back of the cranium
Parietal Bones (2)	Sides and crown of the cranium
Frontal Bone	Forehead
Temporal Bones (2)	Sides of the head near the ears
Ethmoid Bones	Part of the nasal cavities between the eye sockets
Sphenoid Bones	Sides of the eye sockets

The face is composed of 14 bones, nine of which are important in esthetics:

Bones	Location
Nasal Bones (2)	Bridge of the nose
Lacrimal Bones (2)	Inside portion of eye socket
Zygomatic Bones (2)	Cheeks
Maxillae (2)	Upper jaw
Mandible	Lower jaw

The main bones of the neck are the hyoid bone and cervical vertebrae. The **hyoid bone** is found at the base of the tongue, is U-shaped, and supports the tongue and its muscles. The **cervical vertebrae** are a collection of seven bones that make up the top part of the vertebral column.

The chest, or thorax, is the area between the neck and abdomen that consists of the sternum, ribs, and thoracic vertebrae. It protects the internal organs in that area including the heart and lungs. There are 12 **ribs** that comprise the outer cage of the thorax. The **scapulae**, also known as the shoulder blades, are the triangular-shaped bones of the shoulder. The **sternum** forms the front support of the ribs and is sometimes called the breastbone. The **clavicle**, or collarbone, joins the sternum to the scapula.

Starting from the tips of the fingers and moving upwards, the bones of the hands and arms are as follows:

- **Phalanges**: The bones of the fingers, also referred to as digits. Each finger has 3 phalanges, except for the thumb which has 2.
- **Metacarpal bones**: The long, slender bones of the hand that connect the phalanges to the carpus. This region is called both the metacarpus and the palm.
- **Carpals**: Eight small, irregular bones that form the carpus (wrist). The carpus is a flexible joint where the bones are held together by ligaments.
- **Radius**: The smaller bone of the forearm on the same side as the thumb. The radius connects the wrist to the elbow.

29

- **Ulna**: The larger bone of the forearm on the same side as the pinky. Alongside the radius, the ulna connects the wrist to the elbow.
- **Humerus**: The uppermost and largest bone of the arm that runs from the elbow to the shoulder where it connects to the scapula.

The **skeletal system** provides the physical structure of the body. In an adult, it is composed of 206 bones that protect organs, act as anchor points for ligaments and muscles, and provide a framework for the tissues of the body. Muscles are connected to bones by tendons, while ligaments connect bones to other bones. Areas where bones meet are referred to as **joints**. Joints may be **movable**, like those of the hips, knees, and elbows, or **immovable**, like those in the skull or pelvis that allow for little or no movement. Bones in the skeletal system also produce blood cells in their marrow and store the majority of the body's calcium phosphorus, magnesium, and sodium. Understanding the skeletal system allows an esthetician to better perform makeup application, restrict treatment to permitted areas (many states do not allow estheticians to treat areas lower than the seventh cervical vertebrae), and protect their own body while working.

The **integumentary system** is the skin and its accessory organs which includes nails, hair, and sweat and oil glands. The name is derived from the word *integument*, which means natural covering, and refers to the skin and its appendages as the covering for the body. The **skin** is the largest organ of the body. It acts as a barrier system to protect the internal elements of the body from outside factors such as bacteria, injury, and exposure to sunlight. Nails also act in a protective capacity for the soft skin of the fingernail and toenail beds. Hair functions to preserve body heat, prevent debris from entering orifices, and decrease the amount of light that enters the eyes. Sweat glands regulate body temperature by releasing or retaining body heat and oil glands release sebum to protect the skin from friction and dehydration. The integumentary system allows the body to eliminate waste through perspiration while retaining bodily fluids. The integumentary system comprises several miles of blood vessels, millions of glands, and a variety of nerve networks. Skin composition includes proteins and peptides formed from chains of amino acids. Healthy skin is smooth, soft, and slightly moist. An esthetician plays a large role in maintaining client skin health. Therefore, they must understand the composition of the skin and its role in the integumentary system.

The muscular system allows the body to move through stretching and contraction of muscles. The human body contains over 630 muscles. There are three types of muscle tissue:

- **Skeletal**: Also known as voluntary muscles, which contract with conscious thought.
- **Smooth**: Also known as involuntary muscles, which are not under conscious control.
- **Cardiac**: These muscles are specific to the heart and its functions.

30

When providing massage services, estheticians work the skeletal muscles. Skeletal muscles consist of an origin, **belly**, and **insertion**. The **origin** of a muscle is the less movable attachment point to a bone. It is able to flex but remains stationary on the bone. The **belly** is the middle portion of the muscle between the origin and insertion. The **insertion** is at the opposite end of the muscle from the origin. It is the more movable attachment point to a bone. Current best practice is for a massage to begin at insertions and move toward origins while establishing a general pattern of movement toward the heart.

There are four muscles in the scalp:

Muscle	Function
Frontalis	Raises eyebrows, draws the scalp forward, and causes forehead wrinkles
Occipitalis	Draws the back of the scalp downward
Temporalis (2)	Runs along either side of the scalp and allows the mandible to move

The frontalis and occipitalis work together to cover the scalp, known as the **epicranius** or **occipitofrontalis**.

The muscles of the eyebrow are:

Muscle	Function
Corrugator	Draws the eyebrows down and wrinkles forehead vertically
Orbicularis oculi	Closes the eyes
Levator palpebrae superioris	Controls the eyelids

The nose consists of two primary muscles:

Muscle	Function
Procerus	Lowers the eyebrows
Nasalis	Opens the aperture of the nose, known as nasal flaring

The corrugator of the eyebrow and the procerus of the nose form the **glabella**. This area directly above the nose and between the eyebrows is a common injection site for neuromodulators, such as Botox, which inhibit muscle movement.

The muscles of the mouth include:

Muscle	Function
Buccinator	Compresses the cheeks and expels air between the lips
Triangularis	Also known as the depressor anguli oris. Pulls down the corners of the mouth
Mentalis	Elevates the lower lip and raises the skin of the chin

Muscle	Function
Orbicularis oris	Compresses, contracts, puckers, and wrinkles the lips
Levator anguli oris	Elevates the corners of the mouth, such as in smiling
Risorius	Draws the corners of the mouth out and back when smiling
Levator labii superioris	Also known as the quadratus labii superioris. Lifts the upper lip and wings of the nose
Zygomaticus	Pulls the mouth upwards in facial expressions. Also known as "the laughing muscle"

There are two muscles that work together in chewing, the **masseter** and the **temporalis**. They contract to powerfully close the jaw.

The ear consists of three muscles: the **auricularis superior**, **anterior auricularis**, and **auricularis posterior**. They work together to move the ears upward, forward, or backward. The neck consists of two muscles. The **platysma** extends from the chest and shoulders to the side of the chin and lowers the jaw and lip. The **sternocleidomastoid** (SCM) extends from the ear, down the neck, to the collarbone. It is used to turn the head. The shoulder and arm muscles begin with the **trapezius**. It is located along the back of the neck and shoulders where it stabilizes the scapula and allows for shrugging. The **biceps** lift the forearm, move the elbow, and rotate the palms. The **deltoid** allows the arms to extend out and down. The **triceps** cover the back of the arm and allow forearm extension. The arms are attached to the body at the chest by three muscles. The **latissimus dorsi** covers the lower back and extends upward where it rounds forward to attach to the upper part of the humerus. The **pectoralis major** and **pectoralis minor** are the muscles in the chest that allow the arms to move and swing.

Muscles throughout different parts of the body can move in different ways. These movements include:

- **Abduction**: Moves a limb or other appendage away from the body. Spreading fingers and toes apart, and raising the arms so they are parallel to the floor are examples.
- **Adduction**: Moves a limb or other appendage back towards the body and is the opposite of abduction. Bringing the fingers and toes back together after spreading or returning arms to their resting position beside the body are examples of adduction.
- **Flexion**: Bending movements, such as moving the forearm up at the elbow or closing the hand into a fist, are examples of flexion. For body parts that can move forward or backward, such as the trunk, flexion moves them forward.
- **Extension**: A straightening movement, the opposite of flexion. For body parts that can move forward and backward, such as the trunk, extension moves them backward.

- **Pronate**: Muscles are turned inward, such as when the palm faces downward.
- **Supinate**: Muscles rotate outward, the opposite of pronate, such as when the palm is turned upwards.

The **nervous system** is a network of cells and fibers responsible for controlling all functions of the body. The nervous system is separated into three subdivisions:

- **Central nervous system**: The brain, spinal cord, spinal nerves, and cranial nerves make up this portion of the nervous system. It controls involuntary functions such as the five senses and voluntary functions like body movements and facial expressions.
- **Peripheral nervous system**: This system of nerves connects the outer parts of the body to the central nervous system and transmits impulses. This allows information to be relayed between the brain and body.
- **Autonomic nervous system**: All smooth muscles, glands, and blood vessels are controlled by the autonomic nervous system. This system controls the muscles responsible for actions like breathing, moving blood through the body, and digesting.

The **brain**, which is made of nerve tissue, controls the nervous system by sending impulses. The **brainstem** connects the spinal cord to the brain and controls breathing, heartbeat, and blood pressure. The **spinal cord** is a continuation of the brainstem and extends down the trunk. Spinal nerves extend from the cord to the muscles and skin of the trunks and limbs to spread impulses throughout the body.

Nerves are bundles of nerve fibers joined by connective tissue. They originate in the brain and spinal cord and extend throughout the body. Impulses are transmitted through nerves. There are two types of nerves:

- **Sensory nerves**: These nerves work with the sense organs and carry impulses related to touch, smell, taste, sound, sight, pain, pressure, cold, and heat. The endings of sensory nerves are called receptors and are located close to the surface of the skin.
- **Motor nerves**: These nerves carry impulses between the brain and muscles and are used to move the body. **Reflexes** occur when a sensory receptor sends an impulse through the nervous system, which in turn causes an automatic nerve reaction which causes a movement. The most common example is quickly withdrawing one's hand when touching something hot. Reflexes do not have to be learned as they are automatic and involuntary.

There are 12 pairs of cranial nerves located at the back of the brain. They send impulses between the brain and the head, face, and neck. Estheticians should be familiar with nerves V, VII, and XI.

The **fifth cranial nerve** is known as the **trifacial** or **trigeminal** nerve. It is the largest cranial nerve and provides sensory input to the face. It is divided into three branches:

Branch	Area Affected
Ophthalmic Nerve	Skin of the forehead, upper eyelid, interior portion of scalp, orbit, eyeball, and nasal passage
Mandibular Nerve	Muscles of the chin and lower lip
Maxillary Nerve	Upper part of the face

These branches contain several nerves. The nerves affected by facial and lymphatic massage are:

Nerve	Area Affected
Auriculotemporal Nerve	External ear and skin above the temple
Infraorbital Nerve	Lower eyelid, side of nose, upper lip, and mouth
Infratrochlear Nerve	Membrane and skin of nose
Mental Nerve	Skin of the lower lip and chin
Nasal Nerve	Tip and lower sides of the nose
Supraorbital Nose	Forehead, scalp, eyebrow, and upper eyelid
Supratrochlear Nerve	Skin between the eyes and upper side of the nose
Zygomatic Nerve	Muscles of the upper part of the cheek

The seventh cranial nerve is known as the **facial nerve**. It begins at the lower part of the ear and extends downward to the muscles of the neck. The branches of this nerve control the muscles used in facial expressions and secreting saliva. The most important of these branches are:

Nerve	Area Affected
Buccal Nerve	Muscles of the mouth
Cervical Nerve	Side of the neck and the platysma muscle
Posterior Auricular Nerve	Muscles behind the ear

The eleventh cranial nerve, also known as the accessory nerve, is responsible for the motion of the neck and shoulders. The muscles controlled by these nerves are often addressed in facial massage. These nerves include:

Nerve	Area Affected
Buccal Nerve	Muscles of the mouth
Cervical Nerve	Side of the neck and the platysma muscle
Posterior Auricular Nerve	Muscles behind the ear

Nerve	Area Affected
Cervical Cutaneous Nerve	Front and sides of the neck
Greater Auricular Nerve	Face, ears, neck, and parotid gland
Greater Occipital Nerve	Upper Scalp
Smaller Occipital Nerve/Lesser Occipital Nerve	Lower scalp and muscles behind the ear

Restricting or irritating the nerves in the arms or hands can cause them to become inflamed, resulting in numbness, tingling, and discomfort. As arm and hand massages are commonly performed by estheticians, they must understand the location of these nerves. The nerves in this region include:

- **Digital Nerve**: In the palm of the hand and fingers, supplies sensory input to the fingers
- **Radial Nerve**: Runs along the posterior arm and forearm, supplies sensory input to the thumb side of the arm and the back of the hand
- **Median Nerve**: Runs through the anterior portion of the arm and forearm, supplies sensory input to the arm and hand, and is smaller than the digital and radial nerves
- **Ulnar Nerve**: Runs from the neck down into the hand, supplies sensory input to the pinky finger side of the hand and palm

The **vagus nerve** is part of the autonomic nervous system. It runs from the brain through the face and thorax to the abdominal cavity. The vagus nerve controls a variety of internal organ functions such as heart rate, respiratory rate, and digestion. It is also responsible for some reflex responses like coughing, swallowing, vomiting, and sneezing. This nerve can be triggered by stress, pain, or fear. If it becomes overstimulated, it can cause a sudden drop in blood pressure leading to feelings of lightheadedness and, in some cases, fainting. Standing up too quickly, the sight of blood, pain, and pressure on the eyes, throat, or sinus cavity are common causes of overstimulation that occur in salon and spa settings.

The **circulatory system** controls the circulation of blood throughout the body through the heart and blood vessels. It is also referred to as the **cardiovascular system**. The **heart** is controlled by the vagus nerve and other autonomic nerves. It pumps blood through the circulatory system using two circulation systems. **Pulmonary circulation** carries blood from the heart to the lungs where it will become oxygenated. **Systemic circulation**, known also as general circulation, carries the oxygenated blood through the body. Blood travels through the body in a system of tube-like structures called **blood vessels**. There are three types of blood vessels:

- **Arteries**: Thick, muscular tubes that carry oxygenated blood away from the heart to the arterioles (smaller arteries that carry blood to the capillaries)
- **Veins**: Thin vessels with cuplike valves that force blood to flow in one direction. This ensures blood is carried back to the heart for oxygenation and recirculation.
- **Capillaries**: Small, thin blood vessels that connect arteries to **venules** (small vessels that collect blood from capillaries and drain it into the veins). These bring nutrients to the cells and help to remove cell waste materials.

Blood is the vital fluid moved through the body by the circulatory system. It is responsible for carrying water, oxygen, nutrition, and minerals to cells and tissues. Blood also enables the removal of waste products and carbon dioxide by transporting them to the organs that eliminate them. Blood also contains white blood cells, which fight infection and promote clotting of damaged vessels. Blood also helps to regulate body temperature to protect against extreme heat or cold. Blood is composed of:

- **Red blood cells**: Carry oxygen to body tissues
- **White blood cells**: Destroy microorganisms that carry disease
- **Platelets**: Prevent and stop bleeding
- **Plasma**: The fluid component of blood

The main avenues of blood supply to the head, face, and neck are the **common carotid arteries** that run through the neck and split on either side of the throat. Blood leaving the head, face, and neck travel through the **jugular veins** that run parallel to the arteries.

The **lymphatic system**, a component of the **immune system**, contains:

- **Bone marrow**: A primary lymphoid organ responsible for producing the majority of immune system cells
- **Liver**: Creates enzymes needed for digestion, blood detoxification, synthesizes protein, regulates blood sugar levels, and produces several hormones vital to body functions
- **Lymph**: A colorless fluid that circulates in the body. It contains white blood cells and nutrients for cells and absorbs cell waste and toxins.
- **Lymph nodes**: Large, gland-like structures that fight infection and detoxify the blood. The **spleen** is a large lymph node that controls the level of white blood cells, red blood cells, and platelets.
- **Thymus**: A small organ in the upper chest that produces white blood cells

This system protects the body from disease by developing immunity to pathogens and destroying microorganisms that cause disease. It also drains excess **interstitial fluid**, the fluid that surrounds cells and contains nutrients and waste, from tissue.

Unlike the circulatory system, the lymphatic system does not have its own pumping mechanism and relies on the circulatory system to help muscles to move lymphatic fluid. Estheticians can assist movement of lymphatic fluid by providing lymphatic massage.

The **endocrine system** is a set of glands that controls many important functions including growth, development, reproduction, and metabolism. **Endocrine glands** secrete hormones directly into the bloodstream. **Hormones** are signaling molecules that stimulate bodily functions. Examples include estrogen, testosterone, insulin, and adrenaline. The glands of the endocrine system include:

- **Pineal gland**: Secretes the sleep hormone melatonin, and impacts sexual development and metabolism
- **Pituitary gland**: The most complex gland. Secretes hormones that regulate metabolism, growth, sexual maturation, reproduction, blood pressure, and many other functions
- **Thyroid gland**: Secretes hormones that regulate metabolism, heart function, digestive function, muscle control, brain development, and maintenance of bone mass
- **Parathyroid gland**: Secretes hormones that regulate calcium and phosphorus levels in the blood
- **Pancreas**: Produces digestive enzymes that break down carbohydrates, fats, and proteins
- **Adrenal glands**: Secrete hormones that regulate metabolism, stress response, blood pressure, and the immune system
- **Ovaries**: Function in sexual reproduction and determine female sexual characteristics
- **Testes**: Function in sexual reproduction and determine male sexual characteristics

The **reproductive system** is composed of the male and female organs necessary for sexual reproduction. The female reproductive system consists of the ovaries, fallopian tubes, uterus, cervix, and vagina. The male reproductive system consists of the testes, prostate gland, vas deferens, penis, and urethra. The reproductive system produces estrogen, the dominant hormone in females, testosterone, the dominant hormone in males, and progesterone. Hormonal changes caused by the reproductive system impact the skin. Clients experiencing puberty often suffer from acne and oily skin. Clients who are aging, especially women experiencing menopause, experience loss of collagen and elastin in the skin, leading to signs of aging. Female clients who experience a menstrual cycle may notice changes in their skin throughout their cycle, including increased oil production and acne before beginning menstruation. Changes in the hormones produced by the reproductive system can cause clients entering puberty to experience body hair growth. Aging individuals may experience loss of hair on the scalp, growth of unwanted facial hair, and changes in hair color and texture.

The **respiratory system** brings oxygen into the body and expels carbon dioxide through a process known as **respiration**, known more simply as breathing. When breathing in air, oxygen is absorbed into the blood. This process is called **inhalation**. When breathing out, carbon dioxide is expelled. This process is called **exhalation**. The primary components of the respiratory system are:

- **Mouth and nose**: Pull air into the body through inhalation and expel carbon dioxide through exhalation
- **Sinuses**: Cavities that humidify, filter, and warm inhaled air, and produce mucus to prevent infection
- **Pharynx**: Also referred to as the throat, a tube that delivers air from the mouth and nose to the trachea
- **Trachea**: Also referred to as the windpipe, a structure that connects the pharynx and lungs
- **Bronchial tubes**: Small tubes that connect the trachea to the lungs
- **Lungs**: Made of a spongelike tissue that performs gas exchange to process oxygen and expel carbon dioxide

The respiratory system is housed in the chest where it is protected by the ribs. The **diaphragm**, the major muscle group of the respiratory system, is located beneath the lungs at the bottom of the rib cage and facilitates breathing.

The **digestive system** uses enzymes to break down food into nutrients. Nutrients are converted to a soluble form that is transported through the bloodstream and used by cells and tissues. The remaining products that are not absorbed become waste. This system has five major functions:

- **Ingestion**: Referred to as eating, or taking food into the body
- **Peristalsis**: Involuntary muscle contractions that move food through the digestive tract
- **Digestion**: Breakdown of food once it has entered the body
- **Absorption**: Digested foods are absorbed into the circulatory system for cells and tissues to use as energy
- **Defecation**: Elimination of solid waste from the body

Issues in the digestive system or an unbalanced diet can cause nutritional deficits that impact hormone producing glands that then impact the appearance of the skin. For example, the thyroid requires iodine to function. If iodine is not consumed or properly digested by the body, the thyroid cannot produce the hormones needed for basic functioning, which will negatively impact the skin.

The metabolic processes performed within cells create toxins in the form of waste products. The **excretory system** removes these toxins from the body. Waste products can be removed as gas (carbon dioxide), liquid (urine or sweat), or solid (excrement). If this system is not properly functioning, toxins can build up, resulting in negative health consequences. Five main organs participate in waste removal:

- **Kidneys**: Excrete urine, which removes water and waste products from the body
- **Liver**: Discharges bile, which breaks down fats
- **Skin**: Salt and minerals are eliminated through perspiration
- **Large intestine**: Removes undigested and decomposed food
- **Lungs**: Carbon dioxide is removed through exhalation

These organs also participate in other functions, but are crucial to the function of the excretory system.

Histology and Physiology of the Skin

STRUCTURE AND FUNCTION OF THE LAYERS OF THE SKIN

The skin consists of three layers: the subcutaneous layer, the dermis, and the epidermis. The **subcutaneous layer**, also referred to as the hypodermis or superficial fascia, is the deepest layer of the skin. It is composed of a loose connective tissue known as subcutis **tissue**, or **aditissue**, and is 80% fat. This layer provides a protective cushion to internal organs and muscles, acts as insulation, and stores energy. As clients age, this layer will thin. Clients presenting with thick subcutaneous layers may suffer from an underlying hormonal disorder and should be referred to a medical provider for assessment. Fluctuations in hormones impact fat storage which can be reflected by an increase in acne, excessive oil production or dryness of the skin, and changes in hair growth.

The **dermis** is the middle of the three skin layers. It is also called derma, corium, cutis, or true skin. This layer houses blood and lymph vessels, capillaries, follicles, sebaceous and sudoriferous glands, sensory nerves, and the arrector pili muscles. This layer is responsible for supplying the skin with oxygen and nutrients. The dermis is about twenty-five times thicker than the epidermis and is composed of two layers, the reticular layer and the papillary layer. The **reticular layer** is the denser portion and is composed of collagen and elastin. Breakdown and damage of elastin over time is the primary cause of signs of aging such as wrinkles, sagging, and stretch marks. Elastin and collagen are broken down by UV damage, smoking, and environmental exposure. The **papillary layer** connects the dermis to the epidermis and is composed primarily of collagen. This gives the skin strength and assists in wound healing. The blood vessels and connective tissue in this layer provide nutrients to the epidermis.

The **epidermis** is the outermost layer of skin. It is attached to the dermis by a layer of connective tissue called the **dermal/epidermal junction**. This layer contains nerve endings, keratinocytes, immune cells, and intercellular fluids. It is composed of epithelial tissue that covers and provides protection to the body. The epidermis is composed of five layers referred to as strata, the Latin term for "something that has been laid down." Each layer is named using a Latin term that describes its appearance:

- **Stratum germinativum**: "germination or growth layer," bottom layer
- **Stratum spinosum**: "the spiny cells"
- **Stratum granulosum**: "the grainy cells"
- **Stratum lucidum**: "the clear cells," the thick cells that make up the palms and bottoms of the feet
- **Stratum corneum**: "the horny cells"

Melanin, the pigment that protects against sun exposure and determines skin color, is produced in the epidermis.

Internal factors that influence skin health include:

- **Immune system**: The ability of skin to heal, fight infection, and protect the body are dependent upon efficient function of the immune system.
- **Cell replacement**: Damaged skin cells are relatively more difficult to replace than other cell types. However, some skincare treatments and ingredients can stimulate cell replacement necessary to maintain skin health.
- **Glycation**: Glycation occurs when excess glucose in the skin combines with protein molecules. This damages the protein molecules and makes them unable to function properly in the skin.
- **Aging and hormones**: Estrogen is the most influential hormone for skin health. It exerts anti-inflammatory and antioxidant effects, maintains skin moisture levels, and helps with tissue repair. Estrogen production in males and females fluctuates significantly through puberty. Females experience fluctuations coordinated with their menstrual cycles, and estrogen levels eventually decrease with age.
- **Microcirculation**: Circulation of blood from the heart through the arteries, capillaries, and veins back to heart is called microcirculation. When this process cannot be effectively completed, blood becomes trapped in the walls of the capillaries and can cause inflammatory skin disorders such as telangiectasia and rosacea.

External factors that influence skin health are:

- **Sun damage**: Unprotected exposure to UV radiation damages and kills skin cells. This can lead to weakening of the skin and the development of skin cancer. Some form of sun protection should be used to keep the skin healthy.
- **Free radicals**: Free radicals create an unhealthy state for the skin due to unpaired electrons. They pull electrons from other molecules to balance themselves, causing damage to skin cells.
- **Nourishment**: Nutrients from food are transported through the skin where they nourish the epidermis. Topical products with small molecules are able to penetrate the skin and provide nourishment.

- **Environment**: Climate, humidity, and pollutants damage the cells and tissue of the skin.
- **Hormone replacement therapy (HRT)**: HRT is used to balance estrogen in women experiencing menopause. Estrogen derived from plants or animals is used to replace the estrogen that the body is no longer producing.
- **Lifestyle choices**: Many substances like alcohol, tobacco, marijuana, and other drugs impact skin health. Some drugs alter oxygen intake, while others hinder the function of capillaries and other blood vessels.

STRUCTURE AND FUNCTION OF THE GLANDS

Sudoriferous glands, also known as sweat glands, help regulate body temperature and eliminate some waste through sweating. The base of the sudoriferous gland is a coiled structure called the **apocrine gland**. These are found attached to hair follicles under the arms and in the genital region. Apocrine glands secrete oil when they are activated by stress, anxiety, fear, arousal, and pain. The odor associated with these glands is caused by the interaction of the oil they produce with bacteria on the skin. **Eccrine glands** are found all over the body but are more concentrated on the palms, forehead, and soles of the feet. They have a duct below the skin and a pore that secretes sweat at the surface. Unlike apocrine glands, these are not attached to hair follicles and do not typically cause odor.

Sebaceous glands, also referred to as oil glands, are connected to hair follicles and produce sebum. These glands release sebum into the follicular duct and then onto the surface of the skin. The face and scalp have larger sebaceous glands than the rest of the body. A buildup of sebum can cause acne and clogged follicles.

FUNCTIONS OF THE SKIN

The skin is the largest organ in the human body and has six functions:

- **Sensation**: Nerve sensors on the skin transmit impulses to the brain. This allows humans to feel touch, pain, pressure, heat, and cold. These nerves are most abundant in the fingertips. The ability to feel sensations helps keep the body safe through response to external stimuli. For example, when a hot surface is touched, the nerves signal the spinal cord to act on reflex to move the hand which prevents a burn from occurring.
- **Protection**: The skin acts as a protective barrier for the body. It shields the body from injury and produces oil that prevents disease causing microorganisms from entering the skin.
- **Heat regulation**: The human body needs to maintain an internal temperature of 98.6 degrees Fahrenheit to function properly. The skin responds to external temperatures to help maintain that temperature. Blood vessels constrict and blood flow decreases in response to cold, while sweat is released to cool the body in response to heat.
- **Excretion**: The sudoriferous glands expel waste in perspiration.
- **Secretion**: The sebaceous glands produce sebum that slows the loss of water in the cells.

- **Absorption**: The skin absorbs chemicals, hormones, moisture, and oxygen in addition to topically applied treatments. These act to protect, heal, nourish, and moisturize the skin and body.

Skin Disorders and Diseases

Dermatologists are doctors who diagnose and treat skin disorders and diseases. While estheticians are not able to diagnose, they are often the first person to notice an issue with a client's skin during services. As such, they are responsible for referring the client to a dermatologist to receive a diagnosis before they can provide services or treatments to the area of concern. If an esthetician notices what may be a skin disorder or disease, they must stop or refuse to treat the area until an official diagnosis has been made by a dermatologist or other qualified practitioner. Once a diagnosis has been given, estheticians can provide solutions and treatments for many common disorders including acne, hyperpigmentation, and rosacea. Dermatology offices often have an esthetician on staff to provide treatments for a variety of diagnosed conditions.

While estheticians cannot diagnose skin disorders and diseases, they can help clients by educating them and treating these skin conditions where possible. Understanding these conditions allows the provider to administer the most appropriate and effective treatment. It also allows them to stop services when they notice a potential issue. Being able to recognize a skin disorder will prevent the spread of contagious illnesses and allow the client to seek proper treatment. In some cases, such as when the esthetician has noticed skin cancer lesions, this knowledge may save a client's life. Skin issues can be a sensitive topic for some clients. This requires estheticians to be able to provide sympathetic understanding and tactful explanations along with treatment.

DISORDERS OF THE SEBACEOUS GLAND

Acne is a skin disorder characterized by inflammation of the sebaceous glands. It is known medically as acne simplex or acne vulgaris depending upon the severity. It is characterized by clogged pores caused by excess sebum production, dead skin cells, and the presence of Propionibacterium acne (an acne causing bacteria). These clogged pores can cause one of the three types of acne:

- **Papules**: These are red, inflamed lesions that develop from clogged pores. They can become more infected causing pus to develop, leading them to become pustules.
- **Pustules**: These are lesions filled with pus that developed from dead white blood cells, the body's effort to fight infection.
- **Cysts**: These are raised, hardened nodules of infection that are deeper in the skin than papules and pustules. Tissue develops around the infection and hardens to prevent the infection from spreading.

Because clogged follicles lead to development of acne, estheticians should understand the structures of follicles and how to clean them to prevent and treat

42

development of blemishes. A pilosebaceous unit is the medical term for an entire follicle, which is composed of a hair shaft, sebaceous gland, and sebaceous duct. Follicles can become clogged for a variety of reasons, but most often excessive oil, dead skin cells, sebaceous filaments, or foreign particles become trapped and are unable to escape the opening of the follicle, known as the ostium. These impactions cause bacteria to grow within the follicle resulting in acne, inflammation, and pus production. When these follicles rupture or burst, the bacteria they contain spread across the skin and can lead to development of acne in other follicles. Clogged follicles can be prevented by regular exfoliation, keeping skin clean and moisturized, and ensuring that only sanitized hands are contacting skin.

Understanding the types and causes of clogged follicles allows estheticians to prevent and contain the spread of acne. The types of clogged follicles include:

- **Comedo**: These are noninflamed clogged follicles caused by cells, sebum, and debris. Multiple comedo are called comedones. There are two types of comedo, open and closed. Open comedo are also referred to as blackheads due to dark coloring resulting from oxidation. Closed comedo are also referred to as whiteheads and occur when the opening of the follicle is blocked and there is no oxygen exposure.
- **Sebaceous Filaments**: These are solid threads caused by impacted oil. The filaments block follicles and lead to break outs, most commonly on the nose.
- **Milia**: Milia are small white cysts that form from sebum and dead skin cells. They form under the skin and have no visible openings
- **Retention Hyperkeratosis**: This is a hereditary condition that prevents dead skin cells from shedding appropriately, leading to a buildup of cells. The cells mix with sebum and cause comedones to form.
- **Sebaceous Hyperplasia**: These are harmless yellow-, white-, or flesh-colored lesions found on the skin. They are caused by slow cell turnover rates and reduced androgen associated with aging.
- **Seborrhea**: This is abnormal oiliness of the skin caused by overactive sebaceous glands.

Acne is graded on a scale of 1 to 4. Higher grade of acne is associated with the intensity of the methods needed for treatment. Grade I acne is considered minor and is often referred to as mild acne. It is characterized by comedones and some papules. It can typically be treated with over-the-counter skin care products like medicated face wash and spot treatment. Grade II acne, referred to as moderate acne, presents several closed and open comedones and some papules and pustules. Grade III acne is considered to be moderate to severe, characterized by several comedones, papules, and pustules accompanied with redness and inflammation. Grade IV acne is cystic acne and can only be treated with medical intervention, usually by a combination of topical and oral medications. It is often called severe acne. These cysts may be accompanied by comedones, papules, pustules, inflammation, and often lead to scarring.

While there are many triggers for acne, these are the most common and their treatments:

- **Genetics**: If an individual's parents suffered from acne, it is likely they will as well. While these breakouts are controllable, acne caused by genetics cannot be cured. These types of breakouts need to be treated holistically to see improvements.
- **Hormones**: Fluctuations in androgen can cause changes in oil production that can clog follicles and lead to acne. Treating hormonal acne most often includes some form of exfoliation, manual or chemical, so that oil can more easily escape the follicle. Having clients use antibacterial cleanser and water-based moisturizers at home can also reduce hormonal breakouts.
- **Environment**: Particles in the air, comedogenic ingredients in makeup, and changes in oil production in response to the environment can all trigger breakouts. The exact treatment will depend on the cause, but most cases can be treated using regular facial cleansing and exfoliating and avoiding heavy products.
- **Lifestyle**: Stress can cause a spike in hormone production, leading to more oil production. Other lifestyle choices, such as not showering after the gym or using scented products, can also cause breakouts. These types of breakouts can be treated by lifestyle changes.
- **Cosmetics and skin care products**: Some ingredients in these products can clog follicles and lead to formation of acne. Client education on proper products to use based on their skin type will prevent breakouts.
- **Diet**: There have been several links shown between nutrition choices and acne. However, estheticians should not offer nutritional advice. They may refer clients to individuals qualified to give nutritional advice if they feel this will help treat and prevent the client's acne.

Some cases of acne require treatment using prescription medication. The most common drugs and their side effects include:

- **Adapalene**: Topical peeling agent. Can cause drying, redness, and irritation of the skin as well as photosensitivity.
- **Azelaic Acid**: Acidic agent that cleans follicles. Can cause drying, redness, and irritation of the skin as well as photosensitivity.
- **Birth control pills**: Oral medication that regulates the hormones that impact oil production. The most common side effects are irregular periods, weight gain, and cramps.
- **Clindamycin**: Topical antibiotic that kills acne causing bacteria. It can cause extreme skin dryness.
- **Isotretinoin**: An oral medication for treatment of acne. Due to a long list of severe side effects including depression and suicidal thoughts, birth defects, and ulcerative colitis, it is used as a last resort for severe cases of acne.

- **Spironolactone**: Oral medication that regulates production of oil causing hormones. Can cause irregular periods, breast tenderness, facial hair growth in women, and dry mouth.
- **Tazarotene**: Topical retinoid. Can cause drying, redness, and irritation of the skin as well as photosensitivity.
- **Tretinoin**: Topical vitamin A that causes peeling to clean out follicles. Can cause drying, redness, and irritation of the skin as well as photosensitivity.

Disorders of the Sudoriferous Gland

Being able to recognize skin disorders allows estheticians to develop the most successful treatment plan possible, prevent contraindications, and know when medical intervention is required. Common sudoriferous gland disorders include:

- **Anhidrosis**: A low amount of perspiration due to failing sweat glands.
- **Bromhidrosis**: Foul smelling perspiration caused by bacteria and yeast on the skin. Usually occurs in the armpits or on the feet.
- **Hyperhidrosis**: Excessive perspiration caused by overactive sweat glands.
- **Diaphoresis**: Excessive perspiration caused by a medical condition.
- **Miliaria rubra**: Inflammation of the sweat glands that result in burning and itching. Caused by heat exposure and also known as prickly heat.

Contagious Diseases

The most common contagious skin and nail diseases are:

- **Conjunctivitis**: Also known as pinkeye. Inflammation around the eye caused by infection. This is highly contagious and requires antibiotics.
- **Herpes simplex virus 1**: A viral infection that causes fever blisters or cold sores. Antivirals can shorten outbreaks, but there is no cure.
- **Herpes simplex virus 2**: Genital herpes. There is no cure.
- **Herpes zoster**: Also known as shingles. Red blisters form as a rash caused by reactivation of chickenpox in the body. Antivirals can shorten the outbreak.
- **Impetigo**: A bacterial infection that causes bacteria-filled lesions or blisters. This most often occurs in children and requires antibiotics.
- **Onychomycosis**: A fungal infection that causes thick, brittle, discolored nails. It is difficult to cure but can be treated with antifungals.
- **Tinea**: Fungal infection that can occur anywhere in the body. *Tinea pedis*, athlete's foot, is the most common. Can be treated with antifungals.
- **Tinea corporis**: Also known as ringworm. Characterized by a red, scaly, circular infection. Can be treated with antifungals.
- **Verruca**: Also known as warts and appears as flesh colored, blister like masses. They may disappear on their own or be treated with cryotherapy, electric therapy, chemical peeling, or excision during surgery.

SKIN INFLAMMATIONS

Dermatitis refers to inflammation of the skin. The types of dermatitis include:

- **Contact Dermatitis**: Caused by contact with allergens or chemicals.
- **Allergic Contact Dermatitis**: Caused by exposure and direct contact with an allergen, most often makeup, skincare products, detergents, dyes, fabrics, jewelry, and plants.
- **Atopic Dermatitis**: Chronic, recurring dermatitis.
- **Eczema**: Dry, itchy, and inflamed skin. Flare ups can be caused by a variety of factors such as certain foods, detergents, and allergens.
- **Irritant Contact Dermatitis**: Caused by contact with an irritant, such as an allergen or chemical.
- **Perioral Dermatitis**: Acne-like bumps around the mouth caused by products.
- **Seborrheic Dermatitis**: A form of eczema that appears on the face or head.
- **Stasis Dermatitis**: Ulcerations, itching, scaly skin, and/or hyperpigmentation on the legs caused by poor circulation.

Vascular conditions impact the circulatory system. Common examples and treatments include:

- **Rosacea**: Characterized by flushing, redness, inflammation, and skin sensitivity. Rosacea is not completely understood by medical professionals. As such, only the symptoms and not the underlying disease can be treated.
- **Telangiectasia**: Visible capillaries found on the face. They may be caused by injury, heredity, rosacea, hormonal changes, or exposure to excessive heat or cold. There is no cure. However, it sometimes remits spontaneously or with a treatment plan created by doctors.
- **Varicose veins**: Twisted, enlarged veins, most commonly found in the legs. They can be treated by injection or surgical removal.

SKIN PIGMENTATION

Hyperpigmentation is overproduction of pigment and can present as follows:

- **Melasma**: Symmetrical darkening of the skin on the face caused by changes in hormones during pregnancy or birth control use. Worsened by sun exposure.
- **Lentigo**: Flat, darkened areas that develop from sun exposure. They are sometimes referred to as age spots.
- **Ephelides**: Also known as freckles or macules. Small, flat, pigmented marks on the skin caused by sun exposure.
- **Nevus**: Also known as a birthmark. Caused by abnormal pigmentation or dilated capillaries at or directly following birth.
- **Poikiloderma of Civatte**: Causes the skin to turn reddish-brown and develop a white patch under the chin. Caused by chronic sun exposure.

- **Postinflammatory Hyperpigmentation**: Darkened areas of pigmentation following an injury to the skin, usually dark red, purple, or brown. Most commonly seen as acne heals.
- **Tan**: Overall darkening of the skin caused by an increase in melanin production due to sun exposure. Although tanning is often performed for aesthetic purposes, tans cause visible skin cell damage.

Hypopigmentation is the lack of pigment in the skin, causing white or light spots in darker toned areas. This is less common than hyperpigmentation. Common examples of hypopigmentation include:

- **Leukoderma**: Congenital disorder that causes a loss of pigmentation resulting in patches of depigmented skin. Examples include vitiligo and albinism.
- **Albinism**: A genetic condition in which there is a lack of melanin in the body. This is characterized by having light skin, hair, and eyes. Individuals with albinism have a higher risk of developing skin cancer and tend to be more sensitive to light. Albinism is also referred to as congenital leukoderma or congenital hypopigmentation.
- **Tinea Versicolor**: A fungal condition that prevents normal melanin production that presents as flaky patches of white, brown, or salmon colored skin. Sun exposure causes an increase in growth as it stimulates the fungus.

SKIN GROWTHS

Hypertrophies are abnormal growths. Many are benign; however, some are malignant and can become life threatening. It is important for estheticians to be able to differentiate among these growths to best treat and care for clients.

- **Hyperkeratosis**: Thickening of the outer layer of skin caused by a mass of excess keratinocytes.
- **Keratoma**: A thickened patch of skin. The most common are calluses, caused by pressure or friction on the skin, and corns, when the thickening grows inward.
- **Keratosis**: Thick buildup of skin cells, sometimes scaly or patchy.
- **Keratosis pilaris**: Redness and bumps caused by blocked follicles. Usually found on the cheeks, upper arms, or thighs.
- **Mole**: A pigmented collection of cells that varies in shape, size, color, and texture. Also known as a nevus.
- **Psoriasis**: Red patches of itchy, scaly skin caused by overly rapid replication of skin cells. Usually seen on the scalp, elbows, knees, chest, and lower back.
- **Skin tag**: Small flaps of skin. Commonly found on the neck, under the arms, or chest.

SKIN CANCERS

While there are several causes of skin cancer, unprotected overexposure to ultraviolet (UV) light from the Sun is the most common and preventable cause. UV exposure causes damage to the DNA in the skin resulting in cancer causing mutations. UV exposure is responsible for over 90% of skin cancer cases. Preventing unprotected exposure to UV should start early in life as one severe sunburn during childhood can double the risk of developing skin cancer, specifically melanoma, as an adult. Melanoma is the deadliest form of skin cancer. In addition to sun exposure, tanning beds increase the risk of melanoma by 75% as they use concentrated UV light to cause damage and darken the skin. When a provider notices a potential skin cancer lesion, they should refer their client to a dermatologist. They may choose to refuse or provide services but should avoid the lesion depending on the nature of the service.

Providers may notice abnormalities in the skin while preparing for and providing services. These should be noted, and concerns presented to the client so they may be assessed by a dermatologist or other qualified practitioner. There are three main types of skin cancer:

- **Basal Cell Carcinoma**: The least deadly and most common type of skin cancer, presents as small nodules that sometimes have elevated borders or a reddish tint.
- **Squamous Cell Carcinoma**: Red or pink papules or nodules, may be scaly or crusty, and sometimes present as open sores. These can grow and spread.
- **Malignant Melanoma**: The most serious and deadly type of skin cancer. Black or dark colored uneven, rough, jagged, patches. This spreads quickly and is 100% fatal when left untreated.

When observing skin, providers may also notice actinic keratosis. Actinic keratosis is a precancerous lesion that is characterized by a sharp or rough texture and is pink or flesh colored. These should be pointed out to clients so they can be assessed and treated by a dermatologist to prevent development of cancer.

The American Cancer Society recommends regularly self-checking skin for changes and potential cancerous lesions. These often begin to appear as moles or freckles. When checking these spots, one should follow the ABCDEs of Melanoma Detection:

- **Asymmetry**: Are the two sides of the lesion identical?
- **Border**: Is the border regular in color around the lesion?
- **Color**: Is the color the same throughout?
- **Diameter**: Is the lesion smaller than a centimeter?
- **Evolving**: Is the lesion staying the same shape and size?

If the answers to any of those questions are no, one should seek medical attention. Because estheticians often see the same clients for the same services over time, they may notice changes to lesions in areas that clients themselves cannot see. Being vigilant and noticing abnormalities can save a client's life.

PRIMARY AND SECONDARY SKIN LESIONS

Lesions are any changes to skin tissue caused by damage or injury. Primary lesions are the initial changes in skin and are either flat, immovable marks or fluid filled cavities. Primary lesions include:

- **Bulla**: Large, water filled blisters
- **Cysts**: Sac containing pus or other semifluid which can be drained
- **Tubercle**: Sac containing pus or other semifluid that cannot be drained
- **Macule**: Flat, discolored spot on skin such as a freckle or age spot
- **Nodule**: A solid bump under the skin that is larger than one centimeter
- **Papule**: Elevation of skin that does not contain fluid initially but may develop pus
- **Pustule**: Papule that has developed white or yellow pus and is inflamed
- **Tumor**: An abnormal mass
- **Vesicle**: Small blister containing fluid
- **Wheal**: Swollen, itchy lesion most often caused by insect bites and stings

Secondary lesions are lesions characterized by abnormal surfaces or depressions in the skin. Secondary lesions include:

- **Crust**: An accumulation of dead cells that form over a healing wound, also referred to as a scab.
- **Excoriation**: Small sores or abrasions caused by scratching or scraping.
- **Fissure**: Deep cracks in the skin, usually from dryness.
- **Keloid**: Scarring caused by excessive scar tissue growth.
- **Scale**: Epidermal flakes that are abnormally thin, dry, or oily.
- **Scar**: Also referred to as cicatrix, a raised or indented area of the skin caused by a healing injury or cut.
- **Ulcer**: An open lesion on the skin or on a mucus membrane, sometimes presenting with pus or fluids.

Dermatillomania is a type of obsessive-compulsive disorder that causes an individual to pick their skin in a manner that leads to injury, infection, or scarring. Most often, sufferers pick at blemishes, moles, freckles, existing lesions, and patches of skin with irregular texture. Individuals suffering from dermatillomania do not feel that picking at their skin is painful and find relief in these activities. Many sufferers do not realize they are picking at their skin or may do so in their sleep. Picking is often triggered by stress or anxiety. The cause can only be treated by mental health professionals and treatment typically requires therapy and medication. While this is a mental illness as opposed to a skin disorder, it is important that estheticians know the signs and can correctly identify this disorder. Estheticians can help provide treatment for the scarring and injuries caused by obsessive picking.

Body dysmorphic disorder (BDD) is a psychological disorder that causes individuals to become preoccupied with imagined or exaggerated versions of their existing physical imperfections. This disorder prevents individuals from having a realistic mental image themselves. Some common examples are an individual thinking they weigh far more than they really do or that they have far more acne than what others see. This leads them to believe that they are constantly being viewed negatively by others based on their appearance. Excessive and repetitive behaviors like looking at oneself in the mirror, picking at skin, and hair pulling often accompany BDD. Some sufferers of BDD will seek cosmetic surgeries to fix their perceived or felt flaws. BDD sufferers will often be dissatisfied with their treatments, as they are not seeing the actual outcome, but a perceived one where they are still flawed. BDD can only be treated through therapy and medication.

Understanding common skin conditions and what causes them will help estheticians make informed decisions during treatments. These conditions may be the result of an infection or disease that requires services to be stopped. The most commonly seen conditions are:

- **Furuncle**: Also referred to as boils. These are pus filled, raised abscesses caused by bacteria trapped in hair follicles or glands.
- **Carbuncle**: A group of boils.
- **Edema**: Swelling caused by either an imbalance in fluids or as a response to injury, illness, or medication.
- **Erythema**: Reddening of the skin caused by inflammation.
- **Folliculitis**: Also referred to as ingrown hairs. These are common after shaving and are caused by hairs growing under the surface instead of up through the follicle.
- **Pseudofolliculitis**: Also known as razor bumps. These result from inflammation and present as bumps typically present after shaving that look like folliculitis but do not contain hair under the surface.
- **Pruritus**: Persistent itching.
- **Steatoma**: A benign cyst or tumor filled with sebum, typically appears on the scalp, neck, or back.

Function and Composition of the Hair

STRUCTURE OF THE HAIR AND ITS FOLLICLE

Hair acts as a protective feature for humans. It helps the body retain heat, prevents debris from entering orifices, and filters light to protect the eyes. **Trichology** is the study of hair and related diseases. A **hair follicle** is a mass of cells that form a small tube through which hair grows. The appendages on a hair follicle are:

- **Follicular Canal**: The opening of the follicle from which hair grows.
- **Hair Root**: The portion of the hair that lies within the follicle. It anchors the hair to the cell below the skin's surface.
- **Hair Bulb**: Thick cellular structure that surrounds the papilla. This acts as the base of the follicle and contains the cells that produce hair.
- **Hair Papilla**: The connective tissue that transports nutrients needed for hair growth to the follicle.

- **Hair Shaft**: The visible portion of hair located above the surface of skin.
- **Sebaceous Gland**: Produces sebum that lubricates and protects the skin and hair.
- **Arrector Pili Muscle**: The muscle that opens and closes follicles in response to temperature changes.

GROWTH CYCLES

Hair growth occurs in stages, they are as follows:

- **Anagen Phase**: New cells are produced and form hair and root sheaths while the existing hair is pushed upward, causing visible hair growth. The length of this phase depends on the location of the hair growth. Hair on the head can be in the anagen phase for years, while other areas such as eyelashes remain in this phase for shorter periods of time.
- **Catagen Phase**: Cell division stops during this phase and the hair detaches itself from the papilla. The inner root sheath is lost, and hair begins to become mature and dry. These hairs are referred to as "club hairs" due to the club-like appearance of the base. This is the shortest phase in the cycle.
- **Telogen Phase**: The final stage of hair growth. The club hair from the catagen phase moves up and out of the follicle and is held in place by skin cells, leading to shedding. The follicle remains dormant until the anagen phase begins again.

The three major types of hair are as follows:

- **Lanugo**: This is the soft, unpigmented hair found on fetuses and newborns that is usually shed shortly after birth before being replaced by the other two types of hair. It can also be an indicator of certain diseases.
- **Vellus Hair**: This type of hair is found in the areas not covered by terminal hair, such as on women's faces and necks, the trunk of the body, and backs of the hands. It is usually not notable and sometimes referred to as peach fuzz.
- **Terminal Hair**: This is the long, coarse hair found on the head, brows, lashes, genitals, arms, and legs. Changes in hormones during aging trigger a switch from vellus hair to terminal hair in the aforementioned regions.

ABNORMAL HAIR GROWTH

Hair texture, length, and thickness all vary from person to person. However, it is important to recognize patterns of excessive hair growth as they may be indicators of other issues. Recognition of abnormal hair growth can help to inform decisions on hair removal procedures.

Hirsutism is excessive hair growth on the face, chest, underarms, and groin, especially in women. This is caused by an excess of androgen hormones that can be caused by hormonal fluctuations during puberty, menopause, taking medications, illness, or stress. Eliminating the cause of the androgen imbalance will treat hair growth.

Hypertrichosis is excessive growth of terminal hair where vellus hair should be growing, such as on the abdomen or lower back, or hair that grows in the adult male pattern on those who are not adult males. This type of growth can be genetic but may also occur due to changes in hormones or reactions to medications. Unlike hirsutism, this is not caused by androgen hormones.

Polycystic ovarian syndrome (PCOS) is a hormonal condition in some females. According to the US Department of Health and Human Services, it affects 1 in 20 women. While there are several unpleasant symptoms of PCOS, the ones estheticians may see are:

- Excessive hair growth
- Hair thinning
- Male pattern baldness
- Acne

PCOS cannot be cured, but the symptoms can be managed. Estheticians can provide hair removal and skin treatments. Due to the severity of symptoms and the impact they can have on client self-image, it is important for providers to be conscious of the emotions of their client and react appropriately.

Excessive hair growth may be an indicator of an underlying disease, disorder, or syndrome. **Diseases** are conditions with pathological causes such as bacteria, viruses, or imbalances within the body. Diseases that impact hair growth, such as acromegaly or Cushing's syndrome, are caused by medical conditions related to excess androgen production. **Disorders** are when body functions are performed abnormally, including birth defects or genetic mutations. Disorders related to hair growth include adrenogenital syndrome. A **syndrome** is a group of symptoms that characterize a disease or disorder. Polycystic ovarian syndrome presents with a wide variety of symptoms including unusual hair growth. In addition, Achard-Thiers syndrome, a combination of Cushing's and adrenogenital syndrome, causes excessive facial and body hair growth. Understanding the cause of excessive hair growth will allow an esthetician to make the best decision regarding hair removal methods, resulting in the best, longest lasting outcome.

Basic Chemistry

Skin care should be selected based on a client's individual needs, skin type, and the condition being treated. Knowing the chemistry of products, and the benefits and potential side effects of ingredients, allows estheticians to best treat their client's needs and prevent any negative side effects. Some ingredients in skin care can cause adverse reactions when mixed, so it is important to know the potential outcomes of combining skin care products. Other ingredients may cause side effects including itching, redness, and photosensitivity when not used carefully or used too frequently. Understanding this allows an esthetician to make the best choices of products and to educate their clients on proper use. In addition, estheticians should be able to explain the function of each ingredient to their client as well as proper use and any contraindications. The skincare industry is constantly changing with trends and invention of new ingredients and formulations. Therefore, ongoing education is required for estheticians to continue to offer updated and proficient service.

Chemistry is the branch of science that studies matter. **Matter** is any substance that takes up space and has mass. **Chemical structure** refers to the arrangements of matter made up by:

- **Elements**: The simplest form of matter, containing only one type of atom that cannot be further broken down. All matter is made up of a combination of elements. There are 118 known elements, of which 98 are natural and 20 are synthetic.
- **Atoms**: Atoms are the basic units of matter. They consist of protons, neutrons, and electrons.
- **Molecules**: A chemical combination of atoms. Water is an example of a molecule, as it is a combination of hydrogen and oxygen. Molecules can be broken down into **elemental molecules**, which contain two or more of a single type of atom, or **compound molecules**, which contain a combination of two or more types of atoms.

Physical properties are any property of matter that can be observed without making chemical changes. Some of these are detectable using the 5 senses, but some are more complex. Examples include color, smell, density, boiling point, or hardness. **Chemical properties** can only be observed during a chemical reaction, including acidity, reactivity, toxicity, and flammability.

Physical changes are a change in physical properties, such as freezing, cutting, or breaking an object. In the beauty industry, cutting hair is the most common physical change. **Chemical changes** are caused by changes to the chemical makeup of a substance caused by chemical reactions, such as burning, rusting, or bleaching. This is typically performed by combining or separating elements which lead to new materials or substances. Permanent hair coloring requires combining of chemicals that are to be applied to the hair to induce a chemical change. Understanding the differences in these properties and how they apply to cosmetic sciences will help keep the esthetician and the client safe.

Solutions are a type of physical mixture that can be further broken down into suspensions and emulsions depending on their properties.

- **Solution**: The combination of a **solute**, the substance being dissolved, and a **solvent**, the substance dissolving the solute. Water is known as the universal solvent as it has the ability to dissolve more substances than other solvents. When making solutions, liquids can be categorized as miscible or immiscible. **Miscible** means that the liquids can be fully combined and remain combined, and **immiscible** means that the two liquids will not form a stable solution and will separate. Water and oil are an example of immiscible liquids. When immiscible liquids are combined, they form suspensions.

- **Suspensions**: These are unstable mixtures containing undissolved particles and liquids. Suspensions need to be mixed before use.
- **Emulsions**: A mixture of immiscible substances with the addition of an emulsifier. **Emulsifiers** are chemicals that allow immiscible ingredients to combine in a more stable manner than in a suspension.

Surfactants are substances that allow oil and water to fully mix, making them a type of emulsifier. A surfactant molecule is made up of a head and a tail. The heads of these molecules are **hydrophilic**, meaning they are capable of attracting and combining with water. The tails are **lipophilic**, meaning they can attract and associate with fats, like oils. The head dissolves in water while the tail dissolves in fat causing the two ingredients to combine and form an emulsion.

Oil-in-water (O/W) emulsions occur when oil droplets are emulsified in water, and **water-in-oil (W/O) emulsions** are water droplets being emulsified in oil. In O/W emulsions, the surfactants tails attach to the oil droplets with the heads pointing outward allowing them to combine. These emulsions feel lighter on the skin than W/O emulsions due to oil being completely surrounded in water. In W/O emulsions, the heads of surfactants attach to the water droplets with the tails pointing out. These emulsions tend to feel heavier and greasier on the skin than O/W emulsions.

The most common chemical ingredients in beauty products are:

- **Volatile alcohols**: Alcohols that evaporate easily, such as those in hairspray. These are used for their drying and antimicrobial properties in cosmetics.
- **Alkanolamines**: Alkaline substances used to neutralize acids or raise the pH of another product, used most often in hair coloring treatments.
- **Ammonia**: Used to raise the pH of hair products during coloring treatments. It is a colorless gas characterized by a foul odor that is compounded for use in services.
- **Glycerin**: A solvent and moisturizer characterized by its colorless appearance and oily feel, found in many soaps and lotions. Glycerin is very viscous. It is known to have a sweet taste and is nontoxic.
- **Silicone**: A type of oil used for moisturizing. It is lighter and less greasy than other oils. Unlike heavier moisturizers, silicones are non-comedogenic and will not cause formation of comedones.
- **Volatile organic compounds (VOCs)**: Organic compounds that evaporate easily, often used in nail polishes and removers. VOCs are what give many nail care products their strong smell.

INGREDIENTS

Ingredients found in skincare can be categorized as either natural or synthetic. **Natural ingredients** are those derived directly from nature. **Synthetic ingredients** are produced in a lab setting from chemicals. Some of the terms found on skincare labels include:

- **Natural**: Sometimes also seen as **All Natural**. This term is often used loosely as there is no legal definition, but it is meant to state that the ingredients in cosmetics are derived from nature.
- **Organic**: The ingredients used in the cosmetics were grown in nature without use of pesticides or chemicals.
- **Cruelty Free**: These products and their ingredients were not tested on animals.
- **Vegan**: These products contain no animal ingredients or byproducts such as beeswax, lanolin, honey, or animal-based collagen.
- **Gluten-Free**: This product does not contain gluten-containing ingredients, such as wheat.
- **Hypoallergenic**: This product does not contain ingredients known to cause allergic response or irritation to the skin.
- **Noncomedogenic**: This product will not cause clogged pores.
- **Comedogenic**: There are ingredients present in the product known to clog pores.
- **Fragrance Free**: The product does not have added fragrance.
- **Unscented**: The product has no odor.

The ability of a product to be safe for use as intended, known as product safety, is ensured by the FDA through regulatory acts that require the products to meet safety requirements and labeling standards. Companies marketing products not in compliance with these laws are subject to legal action. While this helps prevent many negative outcomes when using cosmetics, **adverse reactions** are still possible. These are undesired effects caused by the use of a product or ingredient contained in a product such as itching, burning, inflammation, blisters, hives, or rashes. They may appear immediately after exposure to a product or develop days or weeks later. Patch tests, applying a small amount of a product to an inconspicuous area to check for reactions, help avoid adverse reactions on the face or large areas of the body. If a provider is servicing a client and notices an adverse reaction forming, they should discontinue the service, rinse the skin, and apply a cold compress until the skin calms.

Functional ingredients are needed in product formulation but do not impact the appearance of the skin. They act as carriers for the performance ingredients and give products their texture and consistency. **Performance ingredients**, also known as active ingredients or active agents, are those that cause changes to the skin. Some ingredients can act as either functional or performance ingredients depending on the formulation. These ingredients include:

- **Water**: As a functional ingredient, it helps spread performance ingredients and keep solutions stable. As a performance ingredient, it replenishes moisture.
- **Emollients**: As functional ingredients, they place, spread, and adhere other substances to the skin. As performance ingredients, they lubricate the skin and protect the skin's moisture barrier.
- **Color Agents**: As functional ingredients, these enhance the appearance of cosmetic products. As performance ingredients, they are used to change the color of the skin, such as in eyeshadow, blushes, and foundations.

Performance ingredients are those that cause changes to the skin. Examples include:

- **Botanicals**: Ingredients originating from plants. They are derived from herbs, roots, flowers, fruits, leaves, and seeds. Botanical ingredients serve many purposes, but they are most often used to maintain skin health, texture, and integrity.
- **Exfoliators**: Ingredients used to remove dead skin cells. Exfoliators can be chemical or manual. **Chemical exfoliators** such as enzymes, AHAs, BHAs, and retinol dissolve dead skin cells. **Mechanical exfoliators** such as oatmeal, jojoba beads, and beeswax polish or scrub away dead skin cells.
- **Lighteners and Brighteners**: Lighteners are used to improve discoloration and brighteners are used to create a radiant appearance. Lighteners are most often enzyme or chemical based and brighteners are usually botanical based.
- **Nutrition, healing, and rejuvenation**: These types of ingredients are used to heal and repair skin. These include topical vitamins, antioxidants, minerals, peptides, probiotics, and polyglucans.
- **Sunscreen**: These may be **chemical**, carbon-based compounds that absorb UV rays from the sun and release them, or **physical**, mineral based compounds that cause UV rays to reflect or scatter. They prevent burning, premature aging, dark spots, and skin cancer.

Functional ingredients are those needed to formulate and use a product but do not make any changes to the skin. Examples include:

- **Surfactants**: These reduce tension between the skin and the product, allowing it to spread more easily. There are two types of surfactants. **Detergents**, the ingredients that cause foaming and help remove debris from the skin, are found most often in cleansing products. **Emulsifiers**, the ingredients that allow oil and water to mix, are found in the majority of skin care products.

- **Delivery Systems**: These allow performance ingredients to penetrate the skin. There are three types of delivery systems. **Vehicles**, such as water, emollients, and silicones, carry or deliver other ingredients into the skin. **Liposomes** are microscopic bubbles filled with performance ingredients that penetrate the skin and release those ingredients. **Polymers** are small molecules that release ingredients at a slow, controlled rate.

LABELING

The term **toxic** is often used to refer to a substance that is poisonous or in some way dangerous. The reality is that everything can be toxic depending on how it is used and how much is used, even water. The phrase nontoxic was created as a marketing term to make consumers feel better about the products they are using, but it has no real, scientific definition. A better term to use when discussing the potential negative effects of a substance is overexposure. **Overexposure** is sensitivity in some individuals caused by repeated or long-term exposure to a substance. The **overexposure principle** states that every substance has a safe and unsafe level of exposure, and that the danger of the substances is determined by the amount of exposure. Substances themselves carry no harm, and it is the manner in which they are used that presents danger. Understanding this concept and being able to correctly use substances that are commonly referred to as toxic in accordance with their instructions and safety data sheets eliminates the risk of overexposure and the associated negative impacts.

The Federal Drug Administration (FDA) is responsible for ensuring the safety of cosmetics through regulatory acts. They define cosmetics as "products (excluding pure soap) intended to be applied to the human body for cleansing, beautifying, promoting attractiveness, or altering the appearance." The two most important FDA laws related to cosmetics are:

- **The Federal Food, Drug, and Cosmetic Act**: This act set standards for the safety of ingredients found in cosmetics.
- **The Fair Packaging and Labeling Act**: This act requires that product labels list net contents, identity of commodity, and name and place of business of the product manufacturer, packer, or distributor.

These laws regulate safety, labeling, and claims made about cosmetics. By requiring ingredient lists and the information listed in the Packaging and Labeling act, consumers are able to make informed decisions when purchasing cosmetics.

FUNCTION

All skin requires care, and regular application of certain ingredients can maintain skin health. However, not all products work effectively on all clients. Some ingredients are universal, but others are more suitable for specific skin types.

- **Universal Ingredients**: These are appropriate for all skin types and include antioxidants, vitamins, minerals, and physical sunscreen ingredients.
- **Combination Skin Ingredients**: Emollients, humectants, and oil regulators. These are meant to balance hydration by providing moisture and reducing overactivity of oil producing glands.
- **Dry**: Ceramides, emollients, humectants. These are meant to provide moisture and range in heaviness depending on the need.
- **Dehydrated**: Humectants and emollients. These are meant to restore skin hydration and prevent water from escaping the skin.
- **Oily**: Hydroxy acids, light humectants and emollients, oil regulators and balancers, clarifiers, and detoxifiers. These are meant to balance oils in an effort to reduce the activity of oil producing glands, thus preventing oil clogged pores.

Treating clients with skin conditions requires use of specific ingredients. The most useful ingredient types for each common skin condition are as follows.

- **Acne Prone**: Anti-bacterials, anti-inflammatories, oil regulators, retinoids, probiotics, and humectants. These are meant to eliminate acne bacteria, reduce inflammation of existing lesions, and prevent clogged pores.
- **Sensitive/Reactive**: Anti-inflammatories, anti-irritants, ceramides, humectants, emollients, topical probiotics, and essential fatty acids. These restore the skin's barrier to prevent irritation, treat the inflammation from prior irritant exposure, and soothe and heal the skin.
- **Hyperpigmentation**: Anti-inflammatories, retinoids, lighteners, and brighteners. These treat inflammation on the skin while correcting the skin's pigment.
- **Mature/Aging**: Ceramides, humectants, emollients, growth factors, vitamin C, peptides, and retinoids. Many of these ingredients increase collagen, the primary building block of skin cells, and improve the overall appearance of skin. These ingredients also serve to restore the skin and protect from further damage.

Cleansers are designed to dissolve oil, dirt, and products from the skin. They may also contain other active ingredients to treat skin conditions, such as acne or dryness. Cleansers can be waters, gels, lotions, creams, or oils. **Toners** are liquids applied to the skin after cleansing, most often using a saturated cotton pad or by spritzing. Alcohol free toners are also referred to as **fresheners** while toners containing alcohol are called **astringents**. Some toners carry active ingredients to treat skin conditions while others further remove any residue left behind after cleaning. **Exfoliants** are used after cleaning to remove the buildup of skin cells, preventing development of clogged pores. **Chemical exfoliants** remove skin cells through use of active ingredients while **manual exfoliants** scrub them away with physical movement. Masks are concentrated ingredients in some kind of carrier, such as mud, clay, or sheets, which are applied to the skin and allowed to sit for a specific period of time depending on the ingredient and purpose. Examples of treatments provided through masks are hydration, acne treatment, anti-aging treatments, and skin barrier restoration.

Massage products are typically oils, creams, lotions, or gels that are used to reduce tension on the skin and allow the provider to easily glide their hands over areas of treatment on a client. They improve blood circulation, skin hydration, and lymph node activity and enhance the overall appearance of the skin. **Serums** are concentrated performance ingredients formulated to treat specific skin conditions or concerns. Their benefits vary depending on formulation and intended use, but they can address hydration, aging skin concerns, acne, and repair skin. **Ampoules** are small, single use vials of serums. **Moisturizers** are cream and lotion-based formulas meant to create a barrier to prevent loss of natural moisture from the skin. **Hydrators** are different from moisturizers as they attract water to the skin. **Treatment creams** fall into the same family as moisturizers and hydrators as they are meant to moisturize and restore the skin, usually overnight. They are heavier than treatments intended for daytime use and contain active ingredients meant to target and treat a variety of specific skin conditions.

Specialty products are meant to provide targeted treatment to specific areas. Treatments for the skin surrounding the eyes are typically formulated to protect the area's thin, delicate tissue, prevent signs of aging, or enhance the appearance of lashes or brows. Common eye treatments and their purposes include:

- **Eye balms, creams, and gels**: Maintain healthy skin around the eye. These typically contain performance ingredients to address concerns such as wrinkling, and a moisturizing base for hydration.
- **Eye makeup removers**: Cleanse the eye area and remove makeup residue.
- **Eyelash and eyebrow enhancers**: Nourish and promote growth of lashes and brows. Some of these formulations are botanical or peptide based and available over the counter while others require a prescription.

Lip treatments are designed to help the lips retain moisture and prevent chapping and cracking. They also help to restore hydration and improve the overall appearance of the lips.

- **Lip balms, creams, and oils**: Hydrate and soften lips. Some contain active ingredients for effects such as healing, exfoliating, or plumping.

Sun protection prevents damage to the skin's DNA caused by excessive, unprotected exposure to UV rays from the Sun. Failure to use skin protection can cause premature aging of the skin and cell mutations that can cause skin cancer. Skin protection products cause UV rays to be absorbed, scattered, or reflected before they penetrate the skin and cause damage. How long a sun protection product will protect from UV rays is marked by its **Sun Protection Rating (SPF)**. The number in the rating tells how long the product will protect skin from burning when used as directed.

The most common sun protection products include:

- **Basic sunscreens**: Products meant specifically for protection from the sun with no other benefit.
- **Combination products**: Combine sun protection with a daily use lotion or cream.
- **Tinted sunscreen/moisturizer**: A combination product that also contains pigment for a light foundation-like skin coverage.
- **BB Creams**: A combination of day cream, sunscreen, skin covering pigments, age prevention, and skincare ingredients.

ACIDITY/ALKALINITY

Potential hydrogen, most often referred to as pH, represents the quantity of hydrogen ions in a liquid and is used to describe solution acidity or alkalinity. All solutions fall somewhere on the pH scale, which has a range of 0-14. A liquid is considered **neutral** when it has a pH of 7, such as distilled water. Liquids with a pH below 7 are considered acidic, and include vinegar, lemon juice, and battery acid, while liquids with a pH above 7 are **alkaline**, and include baking soda, bleach, and lye. Unbalanced pH levels on skin can lead to dryness, dehydration, inflammation, bacterial growth, and other painful outcomes. For example, a client with dry skin should not be treated with an acidic solution as it will further dry and irritate the skin. Conversely, clients with oily skin will not benefit from alkaline treatments as they cause an increase in oil leading to more acne.

Acids have a pH below 7 and can be used on the skin to fight acne and signs of aging as well as treat dark spots and scarring. **Alpha hydroxy acids (AHAs)** are the most common acids used in the skincare and beauty industry. They are used as a chemical exfoliant and to adjust the pH level of other products to make them more suitable for use. Glycolic acid used in exfoliation, and thioglycolic acid used in perm solutions, are examples of AHAs.

Alkalis, also known as bases, have a pH above 7. They are used to soften the hair, skin, and nail cuticles. The most commonly found alkali in the cosmetics industry is **sodium hydroxide**, also known as lye. This is found in chemical hair relaxers and callous softeners. Alkalis can be extremely caustic and should not be left on the skin or hair for longer than instructed. Special consideration should be taken when using alkali treatments near mucous membranes.

Neutralization reactions occur when an acid and alkali are mixed in equal proportions and form a pH balanced solution that produces water and a salt. Neutralizing shampoos and lotions are used to neutralize hair relaxers. They work by applying an acidic solution to hair that is coated in an alkaline treatment, causing the pH to balance and the chemical treatment to end.

Redox reactions, shorthand for oxidation-reduction reactions, occur when oxidation and reduction occur at the same time. **Oxidation** occurs when electrons are lost, and **reduction** occurs when electrons are gained. These reactions occur simultaneously and lead to chemical changes when providing chemical services like coloring or lightening the hair or applying perm solutions and neutralizers.

Exothermic reactions are chemical reactions that release energy as a product in the form of heat and are caused when more bonds are formed than broken in chemicals being combined. These are commonly observed in permanent waving solutions and nail enhancements. **Endothermic reactions** require energy to begin the chemical reaction. Many chemical treatments for hair require the client to sit under a hood dryer for heat energy to activate the chemicals.

Skin Care and Services

Performing a Client Consultation and Documentation

A **client consultation** is a conversation between the client and provider in which they discuss the client's needs and desired outcomes and how those will be addressed and achieved. Every appointment should begin with a client consultation. This is a crucial step in providing services, as it ensures all parties know what to expect.

To prepare for a consultation, the provider should have a pen and the client intake form ready before they begin asking questions. Depending on the service being provided, they should offer materials to help visualize the outcome of the service including a portfolio of work, a menu of style options, nail or hair color swatches, styling books, or digital images. Consultations should be performed in a dedicated area or a workspace that is free of clutter. The area should be aesthetically pleasing and offer ample space for the client to see themselves in a mirror.

The 10-step consultation method provides structure for thorough client consultation.

1. **Review**: For many services, clients will fill out an intake form prior to the consultation. These should be reviewed and any indicated conditions that may prevent services should be discussed.
2. **Assess**: The provider should perform an assessment to gain an understanding of the needs and wants of their client. This will help the provider establish what services are needed.
3. **Preferences**: The provider should ask probing questions to determine the client's preferences. Examples include preferred nail length, manageability of hair, and desired amount of time to spend on grooming.
4. **Analyze**: The provider should analyze the characteristics of the area on which they will be working. Examples include the condition of the client's nails and cuticles, texture, thickness, and growth pattern of hair, and the state of the client's skin.
5. **Lifestyle**: Some lifestyles can impact how long the effects of services may last. For example, those that perform manual labor and work with their hands should not expect their manicure to last as long as for those who do not perform manual labor. In addition, regular swimming and sun exposure will negatively impact chemical hair services and coloring.
6. **Show and Tell**: This step is especially important in managing expectations. The client should show the provider what they want and vice versa. A client may say they want a "shorter cut," which leaves the length open to interpretation. By showing where they want the hair to be cut, all parties understand the desired length. The provider should avoid using vague terms and use reflective listening skills to gain clarity.

7. **Recommend**: In this step, the provider will make suggestions for services based on the information they have gained from the consultation. Recommendations are most often based on lifestyle, hair, nail and skin type, and face shape.
8. **Upsell**: The provider should offer additional services as add-ons at this time.
9. **Maintenance**: The provider should explain to the client how to effectively manage and preserve any service they might receive.
10. **Repeat**: To ensure both parties have the same expectations, the provider should reiterate what they have discussed and what will occur. They should answer any questions before beginning the service.

Client intake cards, also known as client questionnaires, consultation cards, or health history forms, are questionnaires that ask the client to disclose information that is pertinent to services. This includes:

- Products they are currently using
- Their hair, skin, and nail needs
- Preferences
- Lifestyle
- All oral and topical medications they are currently using or recently stopped
- Any known medical issues
- Skin disorders
- Allergies

All of the information collected can impact services in some way, and knowing a client's allergies and sensitivities will prevent the provider from using products that might cause undue harm. For example, clients using topical retinoids on their face should not have their facial hair waxed due to the increased delicacy of the skin and potential for causing wounds and scarring. Due to the nature of the information collected, providers are obligated to maintain client confidentiality. As such, paper forms should be kept in a locked cabinet or drawer, and electronic forms should be protected by passwords and firewalls.

Clients should be made aware that they will need to arrive early to complete their intake form prior to the first appointment. If a salon uses electronic forms, they may offer the client the opportunity to complete them online before arriving for services. Following use in consultations, these forms should be used as the start of a client service record. The provider should document what services were received and any other pertinent information, such as the formula used to achieve their hair color or the scent preferences for massage products before filing the card. When the client returns for services, the provider can retrieve the form to refresh their memory of what services were provided and of the client's preferences. This information should be referred to during the client consultation before beginning services. After services, the process of noting changes and information repeats as the provider records any changes in treatments and preferences for the next visit.

Client consent forms, also known as consent to treat release, are written agreements in which the client acknowledges the services they will be receiving and any risks they may carry. Before asking clients to sign a consent form, they must review the procedure, what complications are possible, and post-treatment care information. The client should provide their medical history, any products they are using in that area, and any allergies they may have. By signing this form, the client acknowledges that both they and the provider have provided all of the necessary information prior to treatment. They also acknowledge any side effects or complications that may follow or result from treatment. Signing the form indicates that the provider has answered all questions and is not responsible for any negative impacts arising from any undisclosed conditions. Clients must read, sign, and date these forms before receiving more invasive treatments such as waxing, chemical treatments, and facials with extractions. The provider should keep these signed forms on file.

Because many salons and spas run on appointment scheduling, late clients can cause significant delays or interruptions for their own services and those of others. The first step in managing tardiness is having a shop appointment policy. A common policy in the beauty industry is to require clients that are beyond 15 minutes late to reschedule. While many clients are understanding, it may be necessary to explain that other clients will be impacted if they are serviced or that their service will be rushed and not meet standards. In the event a client arrives late and servicing them will not impact others, the client can be serviced but should be reminded about the late policy. As a provider begins to get to know their clients, they will be able to anticipate who will be late to their appointments. In these cases, the provider may want to consider adding a buffer by asking the client to arrive earlier than needed or not scheduling another appointment immediately after their predicted end time.

If a provider believes they will arrive late to a scheduled appointment, they should contact the client or have the receptionist contact the client. The client should be offered the opportunity to reschedule or wait if they are able. On occasion, some clients will arrive on a day or at a time for which they are not scheduled. This can lead to the client feeling frustrated, stressed, or confused. The provider should consult their appointment book and calmly explain when the appointment was scheduled for. If necessary, the provider should offer to reschedule the appointment if it was missed or keep the appointment currently booked. Providing reminder services like calls, texts, or emails to remind clients of the date and time of their service will help prevent scheduling mix ups. The use of appointment cards serves the same purpose, but appointment cards are easily lost.

While the majority of clients a provider attracts will be similar to themselves in age, style, and taste, it is inevitable that they will serve some clients who are different from themselves. Older clients may prefer more formal speech, such as avoiding slang and being addressed by Ms. or Mr., and professional conversation. When initially meeting these clients, they should be treated and addressed with formality. Older clients are often sensitive to the topic of aging, so the provider should take care when speaking about age-related skin and hair conditions and treatment options.

If a client is unhappy with their experience, the provider must first ask questions to understand what has caused the negative feelings. If the cause can be immediately corrected, such as correcting their hair color or cut before other appointments arrive, the provider should do so. For anything that cannot be immediately addressed, the client should be offered the earliest possible appointment. If it is not something that can be fixed, the provider should tactfully explain why. It is important that the provider remains calm and level-headed to prevent any further dissatisfaction.

Client Protection

When possible, disposable headbands or hair coverings should be used to secure client's hair during services. In the event disposable options are not available, a towel can be folded into a drape by following these steps:

1. Fold a towel into a triangle by touching one of the top corners to the opposite lower corner.
2. Place the towel on the headrest with the fold facing down.
3. The client will recline and place their head onto the towel.
4. Bring the sides of the towel to the center of the forehead in a way that covers the hairline.
5. Secure the towel in place and ensure that all strands of hair are tucked into the towel using a disposable spatula or the edges of the fingertips.
6. Make sure that the towel is not too tight, and the client's ears are not bent.

Before beginning a facial treatment, the client should be provided with a robe or spa wrap and slippers and allowed privacy to change. Once they have changed, the provider should assist them onto the table where they will receive services. A bolster should be placed under the client's knees to provide support and relief for the lower back. A clean sheet and blanket should be placed over the client to cover them. A pillow should be provided for the client's comfort. The provider will need to drape the client's hair. This process involves using a towel or spa headband to secure the hair away from the face so that it does not interfere with facial services. It is important to ensure that the draping is not done too tightly, and that all hair is secured. Once the client is properly covered and draped, the provider can begin services.

The safety of clients during waxing must be a priority to prevent the spread of germs, wax residue, and hair from other clients. Tables, chairs, and any other furniture used during waxing services that will come in contact with a client's skin must have some form of protective barrier. This barrier is made from disposable paper sheets or reusable linens that are changed between clients. Paper sheets should be disposed of in a closed trash receptacle after use. Used linens must be placed in a closed hamper or container directly following use. Fresh paper or linens should be applied immediately before servicing a new client.

The general rule for draping is any area not actively being waxed should be covered. Similar to table coverings, drapes may be disposable paper sheets or reusable linen sheets or towels. Changing and disposing of drapes should follow the same guidelines as for table sheets. Clients should be offered disposable bikini bottoms for bikini waxing. This is both to provide modesty as well as to protect sensitive areas.

To maintain sanitary conditions and prevent the spread of infection, many of the items used in waxing treatments are meant to be used a single time before being thrown away. Examples of these single use items include disposable bikini bottoms, cotton rounds, tissues and gauze, hair bands, hair ties, paper drapes and towels, wax applicators, gloves, and wax strips. These single use items should be kept in covered containers when not in use. Once treatment has started, items should be retrieved using clean tongs, not hands. Where single use items are not an option, an EPA registered disinfectant is required for use on non-porous items such as tweezers. Porous items, including linens and towels, must be laundered between uses. Two key points to note for waxing hygiene and safety is that double dipping in the wax is unacceptable and gloves are to be worn by the provider at all times.

As with all other services, providers should begin services by washing their hands and ensuring their hands stay clean throughout the service. This may require the use of gloves or frequent handwashing. No products in their original container should be touched by the provider's fingers. They should use clean, single use spatulas to remove products before using. If more product is needed, a new single use spatula should be used. When using pressed powders, they should be scraped onto a clean palette with a clean spatula before using on the client. Loose powders may be poured onto the palette or dipped out with a spatula. For lip products, a spatula should be used to remove the product from its original container and then it can be applied with a disposable applicator. Mascara should be applied using single use wands. Once a single use applicator has been used, it should be thrown away. Using the same single use item in a product twice is called double dipping and causes the product to become contaminated. Products that are contaminated should be discarded. Makeup brushes, like those used to apply eyeshadow and face powders, should be thoroughly cleaned and disinfected between clients using a product specifically formulated for brushes.

Multi use makeup tools and how to disinfect them:

- **Applicators**: Nonporous applicators can be disinfected after services only if they are not single use. Examples include spatulas, brushes, and wands. Specialty cleaners and disinfectants are available for use on these tools. Following manufacturer instructions, providers should disinfect these tools between clients. This does not apply to porous applicators, such as sponged and sponge tip wands, as those cannot be disinfected and should be disposed of.
- **Pencils**: To disinfect a pencil, it must be sharpened to remove the portion used on a client. The sharpener should also be cleaned and disinfected after each use. Only pencils that can be sharpened can be cleaned for reuse, this does not apply to auto-rollers or felt liners.
- **Palettes**: Palettes should be wiped clean, and all products removed before disinfecting. An EPA registered disinfectant should be used according to the manufacturer instructions.
- **Testers**: Testers should be clearly labeled and kept in the retail area. The same rules for disinfecting other multi use products apply to testers. Disposable applicators should be available for use with testers and clients should be offered assistance to prevent the use of fingers in products or double dipping. Any item that is considered contaminated and cannot be disinfected must be discarded.

Skin Analysis

A **skin analysis** is a process in which the esthetician examines and analyzes qualities of the skin to better understand its needs. Skin analyses typically take place in a facial chair using a bright light to take a closer look at the skin. The client's eyes should be shielded from the light using a mask or cotton pads. When performing a skin analysis, the esthetician initially assesses the overall appearance of the skin and checking for any noticeable blemishes or indicators of infection. They will then palpate the skin to check its elasticity, hydration, and oiliness to determine the skin type. Once this has been established, the esthetician will determine the client's Fitzpatrick skin type. Using the information gathered in a skin analysis with information collected during a client consultation allows an esthetician to select the best products and plan the best services for their client.

Skin types are determined based on individual genetic traits. The four types are:

- **Normal**: Balanced oil and hydration levels, small pores, blemishes are rare, skin is smooth with good elasticity.
- **Combination**: Moderate to high levels of oil, hydration ranges from good to dehydrated, pores are larger in the T-zone (the chin, bridge of the nose, and brow ridge) than in other areas, some blemishes are common, and skin feels oilier in the center than on the sides.

- **Oily**: Moderate to high levels of oil, hydration ranges from good to dehydrated, moderate to large sized pores, blemishes are more common, and skin feels thick, firm, or uneven.
- **Dry**: Minimal levels of oil and hydration, fine or difficult to see pores, and skin is often dull, flakey, blotchy, rough, thin, and/or tight.

Each type of skin requires specialized care to achieve optimal results. Skin types may change over time. Skin tends to become dryer with age, leading to necessary changes in skin care routines.

The **Fitzpatrick scale** is used to measure the skin's ability to tolerate exposure to UV rays. Racial genetics are the biggest influence on Fitzpatrick skin type. There are 6 types:

- 1: Skin is very white, almost translucent, and often freckled. Eyes are blue or green. Hair is blonde or red. Always burns from unprotected sun exposure, does not tan.
- 2: Skin is light. Eyes are blue, hazel, or brown. Hair is red, blonde, or brown. Burns easily, tans minimally.
- 3: Skin is fair to olive. Eyes are brown and hair is dark. Tans well, burns moderately.
- 4: Skin is light brown. Eyes and hair are dark. Tans easily with minimal burning.
- 5: Skin is dark brown. Eyes and hair are dark. Rarely burns, and tans easily.
- 6: Skin is dark brown or black. Eyes are hair are dark. Never or rarely burns and tans easily.

Sensitive skin is easily irritated by exposure to products, the sun, or stimulation. Irritation can be caused by a variety of factors, including genetic predisposition. Individuals with Fitzpatrick type 1 skin are more likely to have sensitive skin due to the thinness of the skin and the close proximity of blood flow to the skin's surface. Skin may also become sensitized due to use of harsh products or medications, and environmental exposures such as heat, cold, or direct sunlight. Due to lower tolerance for abrasive or aggressive treatments, sensitive skin can be more difficult to treat than normal skin. Completing a skin analysis will provide the esthetician with a better understanding of the cause of the sensitivities and allow them to establish the best plan for treating the skin. As a rule, sensitive skin should be treated with gentle, calming products. Extractions and rough exfoliation should be avoided.

Fitzpatrick skin types 4-6 are the most challenging types of skin to treat. They can become hyperpigmented following harsh treatments or aggressive exfoliation, making it necessary to treat the skin with a gentler approach. While clients with this skin type do not typically experience sunburn, sun protection is still needed to avoid hyperpigmentation. Because these skin types are thicker, they produce more oil and need deep cleaning to avoid breakouts caused by buildup in follicles. Waxing may be more difficult on clients with this skin type as they tend to have thicker hair with thicker roots. In addition, clients with skin types 5 and 6 are prone to keloids and hyperkeratosis. Due to the darkness of these skin types, it can be difficult to see reactions to products and treatments. This requires more vigilance from the esthetician to thoroughly check treated areas for signs of adverse reactions following treatments.

The skin that comprises the neck and chest area is distinct in nature from the skin on the face and should be treated differently. The lower neck and chest together are referred to as the décolleté. The neck and décolleté have less sebaceous glands than the face, causing them to age more quickly due to lack of oil production and hydration. This area is equally susceptible to photodamage, broken capillaries, fine lines, and wrinkles as the face. However, many facial treatments are too aggressive to be used in this area. Products containing vitamin A and AHA should be used cautiously in this area. Many treatments for the neck and décolleté area contain antioxidants, growth factor serums, and moisturizers. Clients should be reminded that this area needs sun protection as much as the face does to prevent sun damage and accelerated signs of aging.

There are several factors that can impact the overall appearance and complexion of the skin. These can be categorized as extrinsic or intrinsic factors. Extrinsic factors are the external factors that can negatively impact skin, such as:

- UV exposure from the sun or tanning beds
- Environmental exposure to pollutants
- Climate and humidity
- Misuse, overuse, or lack of use of skin care
- Photosensitivity caused by medications or skin treatments

Intrinsic factors are internal factors that influence the skin. Examples include:

- Genetics
- Free radicals
- Dehydration
- Vitamin deficiencies
- Hormones
- Medical conditions
- Aging and age-related conditions like puberty or menopause
- Glycation
- Pregnancy

Some of these factors, such as dehydration, misuse of products, and vitamin deficiencies, are easy to treat and correct. Other factors including hormones, genetics, and climate cannot be changed easily or at all in some cases. Knowing the presence and impact of factors that cannot be altered allows an esthetician to make informed decisions regarding their client's treatments and skin care.

Contraindications for Skin Services

A **contraindication** is an existing factor that indicates a treatment or service should not be performed on a client, as it could potentially lead to an adverse reaction. Communicable diseases, skin disorders, medical conditions, oral and topical medications being used or recently stopped, and skin irritation or sunburn are all examples of contraindications. All potential contraindications should be listed on client intake forms along with a space to write in any current or recent medications. A provider will need to review this information and confirm its accuracy with their client during the consultation before beginning any service. Performing treatments on clients with contraindications can lead to injury, painful reactions, and medical emergencies. A provider should check for visible contraindications during skin analysis, including cold sores or abnormal skin. Estheticians have the responsibility to refuse services where contraindications exist to protect the client, themselves, and other clients. In some cases, alternative services may be offered to achieve similar results.

Contraindications caused by disorders, diseases, or conditions include:

- **Skin diseases, disorders, or irritation**: Areas presenting with these issues should not be treated. If the client is in good health otherwise, treatments may occur in other areas.
- **Pregnancy**: Pregnant clients should not receive electrical treatments, chemical peels, or use any aggressive treatments without physician approval. Pregnant clients may experience more pain and sensitivity during waxing.
- **Metal pins or plates in the body**: Avoid electrical treatments in the general area of the hardware. Physician approval is needed before treatment.
- **Pacemakers or heart irregularities**: Avoid all electrical treatment that require use of a grounding pad.
- **Allergies**: Avoid allergens during treatment, use fragrance free products intended for sensitive skin.
- **Seizure disorders**: avoid all electrical treatments and light treatments that emit pulsating light. It is best to obtain physician approval before treatment.
- **Autoimmune diseases**: Avoid hard or stimulating treatments.

Contraindications caused by medication or skin treatments include:

- **Use of Isotretinoin**: Clients should not receive skin treatments while taking Isotretinoin, nor for 6 months after final use.
- **Chemical exfoliants and skin thinning topical treatments**: Waxing, exfoliation, and peeling treatments should be avoided while using and for at least one week after discontinuing use.
- **Oral steroids**: Exfoliating, waxing, and stimulating treatments should be avoided during use and for at least two weeks following the end of use.

- **Blood thinners**: Waxing and extractions should be performed with extreme care to prevent tears in the skin that could lead to bleeding.
- **NSAIDs**: Waxing and extractions should be performed with caution as these medications have a blood thinning effect.

Treatment Protocol

Following treatments, all reusable implements should be cleaned and disinfected. Disinfectant in salon disinfectant jars should be changed as necessary in compliance with manufacturer's instructions, and spray disinfectants should also be used in accordance with their SDS. Single use items should be disposed of in a closed container. Used linens and sheets should be rolled so that the side that touched the client is facing inward. These should be placed in a closed container, taking extra care to ensure they do not touch other items in the room. All containers, products, and equipment that were used such as wax pots, steamers, and magnifying lamps should be cleaned and disinfected. The final step in cleaning and disinfecting a treatment room is to clean and disinfect all counters, sinks, work surfaces, and floor mats.

Before beginning any services for the day, the provider should ensure their supply of clean linens is adequate for the services that will be rendered and replenish them if needed. They should turn on any appliances that need time to preheat, such as towel warmers, wax heaters, and table warmers. For each client, the provider will need to prepare the treatment table, which includes first washing their hands and retrieving the linens. The table should be covered with a clean sheet, and a hand towel should be placed at the head of the table with another hand towel laid out to be placed over the neck and décolleté when the client is on the table. A second sheet and blanket are to then be placed on the table for the client to lie beneath, and a headband, gown or wrap, bolster, and pillow should be at the ready. The provider will then set up supplies on their workstation in the order that they will be used. If deemed necessary by the treatment, the provider will arrange a dressing area for the client. After completing these steps, the provider should wash their hands again and prepare to greet their client.

Following treatments, the provider must clean the room and prepare it for the next client. They will first remove all used towels and sheets. Any disposable items used will be discarded into a covered receptacle. If extraction lancets were used, they must be placed in a sharps disposal container. The provider will wipe down all equipment used with an EPA-approved disinfectant. Workstations and trolleys need to be cleaned and reset between uses. They should be restocked with items that were used during the last service. Products used during treatments should be returned to the area they are stored in when not in use. Bowls used during treatment should be washed with warm water and antibacterial dish soap. A clean linen should be placed on the table in preparation for the next client. If it is the end of the day, the provider should unplug all equipment, ensure all necessary areas and items have been cleaned and disinfected, refill containers and supplies, and empty the trash.

For all services, the provider should begin by warmly greeting the client in the reception area. If this is a new client, the provider should introduce themselves. Returning clients should be greeted by name. The provider will then review the client intake form and review what services will take place. They should confirm that there are no contraindications for the intended treatment and have the client sign a consent form. For services that will take place on a treatment table and require the client to dress down, the provider will explain what clothing and jewelry needs to be removed, provide them with a wrap or robe, and indicate the changing area. The client should be instructed on which way to lie on the table. The provider will then place a bolster under the knees if the client is lying face up or under the ankles if they are lying face down. The client's body and hair should be properly draped. After all preparations are complete, the service may then begin.

The structural requirements for a treatment room are:

- **Size**: The room should be large enough to accommodate the equipment needed and movement of the esthetician during services.
- **Proper ventilation**: A variety of fume producing chemicals and treatments are used in treatment rooms and require proper ventilation to not become trapped in the room.
- **Electrical outlets**: The room should be designed in such a way that outlets are easily accessible. There should be a minimum of four outlets per room. Extension cords are both tripping and fire hazards and should be avoided.
- **Washable floors**: Carpet and rugs are not ideal for treatment rooms as they harbor dirt and germs. Tile, stone, bamboo, and other hard floorings are better suited for treatment rooms as they are easier to clean.
- **Proper lighting**: While dim lighting is most relaxing, some treatments require high or low light. Therefore, lighting should be adjustable.

Before beginning an acne treatment, the provider should gather all products needed and wash their hands. A cleanser with both an exfoliating ingredient and soothing ingredients should be used to cleanse the skin before it is analyzed. Once the esthetician has analyzed the skin, they can then steam the face and apply a serum containing exfoliating and soothing ingredients. The esthetician will need to soften the skin through a process known as desincrustation in which the outermost layer of the skin is softened. Once the skin is softened, extractions can be performed, after which an astringent should be applied. A deep cleaning mask is applied, allowed to set, and then removed. This is followed by a soothing mask which is then removed gently with wet cotton. A moisturizer is applied as the final product. Galvanic or high-frequency treatments can be added if desired and appropriate for the client. A post-treatment consultation is the final step in this protocol.

Cleansing Procedures

Cleansers are the first step in most facial treatment routines. They remove makeup, oil, and other impurities, and cleanse the skin to prepare it for other treatments. Some cleansers contain active ingredients that treat skin conditions. The different types of cleansers are:

- **Cleansing waters**: Also referred to as micellar water. Microscopic oil molecules suspended in water that are applied to a cotton pad and wiped across the skin. Made for all skin types.
- **Cleansing gels**: Water based foaming cleanser. These are the most popular types of cleanser.
- **Cleansing lotions**: Light emulsions that clean without stripping away natural moisture. Best for dry to normal skin.
- **Cleansing cream**: Rich emulsions that dissolve makeup and oil. Best for dry, mature skin but also used to ease removal of heavy makeup.
- **Cleansing oils**: Oils that break down makeup and debris on top of the skin. These should be followed by another cleanser to remove the oil.

Toners are a water based liquid product meant to tone and tighten the skin. They are applied using a cotton pad or by spritzing, typically after cleansing has occurred. This allows them to remove any residue left behind from the cleanser and to balance the pH of the skin. They cause the skin to become softer and better able to absorb other products. Many toners have a tightening effect on pores. Fresheners are alcohol free toners containing soothing ingredients meant to calm the skin such as botanicals and hydrators. Astringent toners contain alcohol and may contain other active ingredients such as hydroxy acids. These are formulated for oily and acne prone skin. Due to the nature of the ingredients, the eye area should be carefully avoided when applying toners.

Cleansing the skin is the first step in a facial, as it removes all makeup and debris, softens the skin, and prepares it to absorb the products that will be used. Warm towels can be applied to the skin before cleansing. This will allow the skin to soften and hydrate, making it easier to cleanse. If the client is wearing makeup, eye and lip products should be removed first using makeup remover and cotton pads. Clients who wear contacts should be asked to remove them prior to use of makeup remover as it can run into the eyes and damage the contact lenses. Based on the client's skin type and concerns, the esthetician will select the most appropriate cleanser to use and cleanse the client's face. If makeup residue remains, a second cleansing may be necessary. A toner is then used as the final step in cleansing. Once the skin has been effectively cleansed, the esthetician can complete a skin analysis.

The esthetician should wear gloves for the duration of the cleansing procedure. If desired, a warm towel may be placed on the face for one minute before cleansing. This step is optional but will help soften the skin. Using a cleanser appropriate for the client's skin, the esthetician will spread approximately one teaspoon of cleanser across their fingertips and hands. Starting at the décolleté, the esthetician should apply cleanser from the center outward. After using six passes to cleanse the area, the esthetician will move up to the neck and use their palms to slide their hands upwards towards the ears. They will then reverse their hands and move downwards to the chin. This motion will be continued, moving closer to the center of the face with each movement. Using the pads of their fingers, the esthetician will cleanse the nose and forehead. As a rule, the esthetician's hands should not leave the client's face during the cleansing process. They should only be lifted at the conclusion of cleansing.

Wet wipes, cotton pads, or towels may be used to remove products depending on the preference of the esthetician. Beginning at the center of the décolleté, the esthetician will make outward passes at least three times or until all product has been removed. Once the décolleté is clean, the esthetician will make upward strokes following the same three pass rule. The chin, jawline, and cheeks are wiped next with upward motions. The area under the eye should be wiped from the outside to the center to avoid aggressive tugging of the skin. The area under the nose should be cleansed with a down and outward motion followed by outward movements up the bridge of the nose. The forehead should be cleansed with at least three outward motions from the center leading to the temple. At this point, there should be no product residue remaining and the client is ready for a skin analysis.

Steaming Procedures

Steamers are often viewed as the most important tool in esthetics. There are a variety of models available in different sizes and price ranges with optional features based on the needs of the esthetician. They are primarily used to soften the skin prior to a facial or extractions but are also used to soften masks and aid in their removal. This softening also allows for easier cleansing and removal of built-up dead skin cells and debris. The use of steam can benefit clients suffering from congestion or sinus pain and some steamers have aromatherapy features to aid in calming and relaxation. Newer, high-end steamers often feature ozone, which is a molecule comprised of three oxygen atoms, as opposed to the two oxygen atoms found in ordinary oxygen gas. The third atom allows the oxygen to kill bacteria and microorganisms on the skin. However, overexposure to ozone can be harmful, so caution should be taken to ensure exposure is within a safe limit.

Following best practices and using steamers with caution allows estheticians to provide the best results for clients while also keeping them safe. Steamers should not be used excessively on skin that is red or inflamed, as steaming dilates the capillaries and causes more redness. The steamer should be kept a safe distance from the face according to manufacturer instructions to prevent burns. The steam should be directed evenly across the face for best results, which may require the esthetician to reposition the steamer. Steam treatments should always be supervised because steamers can malfunction and spray hot water, or the water level may drop too low and cause the jar containing the water to burst. This could result in burns or injuries to an unattended client with the esthetician liable. A steamer that has been overfilled may overflow and lead to burns or water hazards on the floor.

Steamers must be filled with water prior to use to produce steam. The water used should be free of minerals and additives as these cause buildup over time. This buildup can lead to hot water sputtering from the steamer causing burns to the client or esthetician. Distilled water is the best choice to use in steamers as it contains no minerals or chemicals. Water should be emptied from the steamer at the end of each day and the jar that holds it should be regularly cleaned. A steamer requires five to ten minutes to warm up and produce a steady stream of steam. Steamers should not be left unattended while they warm up as the water may run low and cause the jar to overheat and burst. Only water should be added to the jar. Essential oils and other additives should only be used with specialized attachments to ensure safety. The outside of the steamer should be wiped with disinfectant after every use.

Exfoliation Procedures

Exfoliant treatments are any product or action meant to remove dead skin cells and other buildup from the skin. They are most often used after cleansing. The frequency of use is dependent upon individual needs and the manufacturer instructions. Exfoliants help create a brighter complexion by smoothing and softening the skin. Removing the dead skin cells and buildup through exfoliation allows the skin to better absorb ingredients in other skin care products. It also allows for pores to be more deeply cleansed and for easier extractions. There are two types of exfoliants. Chemical exfoliants contain ingredients that are meant to eliminate dead skin cells. Mechanical exfoliants physically buff off dead skin cells. Exfoliation treatments should not be used on clients with sensitive, thin, or acne prone skin as they can cause irritation or bruising. Patients using certain topical treatments and medications that contain retinol, hydroxy acids, or other prescription ingredients should avoid exfoliation as it can damage the skin.

Chemical exfoliation uses chemicals such as hydroxy acids, chemical compounds, or retinol to remove dead skin cells and buildup. These active ingredients can be found in serums, cleansers, masks, and creams. Products used in a professional setting contain higher concentrations of active ingredients than those sold for use at home. Enzyme treatments are a gentler chemical approach that use enzymes from plants such as pineapples or papayas to exfoliate the skin. Mechanical exfoliation occurs when dead skin cells are polished from the surface of the skin. This can be achieved through cleansers containing scrubbing agents or masks containing rice bran, almond meal, jojoba beads, or magnesium crystals. Gommage is a combination of mechanical and enzyme treatment. A mask is applied to the skin and allowed to dry as enzymes digest dead skin cells. The mask is then removed, which takes remaining cells with it.

Alpha hydroxy acids (AHA) are mild acids used in chemical exfoliation. AHAs penetrate the skin, loosen the bonds between cells, and stimulate production of lipids. Examples of AHAs include:

- Glycolic acid
- Lactic acid
- Tartaric acid
- Malic acid
- Citric acid
- Mandelic acid

AHAs are recommended for dry or undamaged skin, or skin with mild breakouts. These acids are used as part of a treatment plan and require regular masking and home treatment between visits to an esthetician to produce the best results. Estheticians should create a treatment plan and share it with the client to provide instruction on regular use of AHAs. Most treatment plans start clients with a mild level of peel and work up to stronger peels over time. This helps to avoid any initial dryness or peeling of the skin. AHA peels should not be used on clients using retinol or vitamin A treatments as part of their regular skin care routines.

Beta hydroxy acids (BHAs) are acids used in chemical exfoliants. They are far harsher on the skin than AHAs and are intended for use on oily, acne prone skin. BHA treatments cause flaking and peeling. Therefore, to prevent severe reactions clients should start with a lower strength treatment and work their way up over time. Clients may experience a slight burning or tingling sensation when BHA treatments are applied. This is normal and will subside as the treatment sets. Once desired results have been achieved, clients can be moved to a maintenance plan using lower strength or less frequent treatments. Acid treatments, both in the salon and at home, cause photosensitivity. Clients should be informed of this so they can take measures for sun protection. As with other acid-based treatments, clients using retinol or vitamin A products are not eligible for BHA peels due to increased skin sensitivity.

Microdermabrasion is a machine-based exfoliation treatment. It polishes dead skin cells from the surface of the skin using a crystal spray or diamond tip. It helps to correct the look of sun damage, pigmentation, comedones, fine lines, wrinkles, pores, and textured skin. Microdermabrasion should not be used on sensitive or irritated skin, clients using retinol or vitamin A treatments, clients with any type of skin disorder or disease, or clients who are pregnant. Clients should wear protective eyewear and masks to ensure crystals and dead skin cells do not enter their eyes and extra care should be taken to ensure none enter the mouth or nose. The types of microdermabrasion are:

- **Crystal microdermabrasion**: Microcrystals are sprayed on the surface of the skin, then vacuumed off.
- **Crystal-free microdermabrasion**: A diamond tip applicator is used to polish the top layers of skin.

- **Hydradermabrasion**: Also known as wet microdermabrasion. An abrasive tip is used to apply serum to the skin. The serum is collected using the machine's handpiece. A tip designed for penetration is then used on the skin.

Basic Massage Movements

Effleurage is the most important of the five basic massage movements. It is used at the beginning and end of a facial massage and aids in relaxation. The palms and fingers are used to softly perform slow, continuous strokes across the skin. This is typically done with medium pressure but can be altered to fit the needs of the client. Effleurage is used to massage the forehead, face, scalp, shoulders, neck, chest, arms, and hands. The pads of the fingers are used on small areas while the palms are used on larger areas. The hands should be kept loose and relaxed with the fingers curved to conform to the area being massaged. Once this type of massage has begun, the esthetician's hands should never leave the area being massaged and should only be removed when massaging that area has concluded.

Pétrissage is a massage technique that uses kneading, squeezing, and pinching to compress the deeper muscle tissue in the face. The skin and flesh are grasped between the forefinger and thumb, lifted away from the underlying structure, then squeezed, rolled, or pinched using light to firm pressure to stimulate the tissue. Massage movements should be rhythmic and flow thoughtfully across the areas being worked. This type of massage can be performed on the face, shoulders, and arms to promote circulation, resulting in better skin tone and overall appearance. Pétrissage is especially beneficial in the shoulder area where muscle knots are common. It is also used to promote lymphatic drainage and the draining of toxins from the skin. As it is more aggressive than other methods of massage, pétrissage should not be used on clients with inflamed, irritated, broken, or swollen skin.

Tapotement massage, also known as percussion massage, uses the fingertips to rapidly tap the skin. The movement used is sometimes called piano movement. Tapotement is performed with the pads of the fingers, not the fingertips as the fingernails may scratch or injure a client. This type of massage improves circulation through stimulating the capillary network and releasing nutrients that help to nourish the skin. It also releases carbon dioxide and waste materials to purify the skin's system. Tapotement leads to an overall toned appearance of the skin and is especially helpful for improving the appearance of sluggish skin. It should be used carefully, as it is the most stimulating of the five facial massage techniques. Special care should be taken on the face where only a light tapping movement should be used. Stronger taps may be used on other parts of the body during a facial massage, like the chest and shoulders.

Friction facial massage uses a rubbing technique to stimulate the skin to increase circulation and glandular activity, thereby improving the skin's appearance. Friction massage is performed using the pads of the fingers to create either circular or crisscross motions. Light friction should be used on the face and neck with a deeper pressure applied to the scalp, arms, and hands.

In vibration massage, the esthetician applies the balls of their fingertips to the desired point of application and begins rapidly shaking the area by quickly contracting the muscles in their arms. This method of massage is the most stimulating and should only be used for a few seconds in each carefully selected area. Vibration increases circulation, helps with draining, improves the elasticity of the skin, and relieves muscular tension.

The most common facial massage techniques are derived from Swedish massage. However, there are other methods of massage that are equally beneficial during facials.

- **Acupressure**: Derived from Chinese medicine. Pressure is applied to acupressure points to help release muscle tension and restore balance to the body. Acupressure is thought to stimulate *chi*, which Chinese medicine sees as the life force and energy of the body.
- **Shiatsu**: Derived from Japanese massage techniques. Acupressure points are massaged to relax and balance the body.
- **Pressure point**: Similar to acupressure. Inward pressure is applied to each pressure point for three to six seconds before moving to the next point.
- **Aromatherapy massage**: Essential oils are combined with massage oil and applied to the body. The scents are meant to promote mental relaxation.
- **Manual lymph drainage (MLD)**: Gentle pressure is applied to the lymphatic system to aid in draining. This helps to reduce swelling.

Choosing the proper starting point is a technical skill that will vary based on the service. Massages can begin on the chin, décolleté, or forehead. Similarly, the amount of pressure used will vary based on client preference and the sensitivity of the area being massaged. Muscles should be massaged from insertion, the portion of muscle attached to a moveable area like a joint or bone, to origin, the portion of muscle attached to the immovable part of the skeleton. While the massage products used will vary based on the needs of the client, they are a crucial part of massage services as they help to reduce friction and allow the hands to glide across the skin.

While some aspects of massage will vary based on the desired outcome, there are a few skills that apply universally. Once the esthetician has placed their hands on the client's skin to begin the massage, they should not be removed until it is time to conclude services. Removing the hands causes a disruption in the massage and can inhibit the client's relaxation. While massaging, hand movements should flow logically and glide from one area to the next. It is important that the esthetician communicates with the client so that they can adjust the pressure they are using to best suit the client's needs.

Methods of Extraction

Extraction is manual removal of a comedone from a follicle. This is often the only way to eliminate a comedone from a follicle and allow the follicle to return to its normal size. In some cases, lancets are used to open papules and pustules to allow the trapped pus to drain. Use of a lancet is not permitted in all states. Therefore, it is required that the esthetician be knowledgeable of their state's regulations. Before beginning an extraction, the esthetician should wash their hands and put on gloves, as this procedure is invasive. The client's eyes should be covered to protect them from the magnifying lamp placed over their face. The esthetician will use the magnifying lamp throughout the service to ensure they are removing all debris. Any debris or fluids left behind will lead to more clogged follicles. Comedones can be removed using the manual removal method of the esthetician's fingers wrapped in gauze, the cotton swab technique, a comedone extractor, or lancet where permitted.

Once a client's skin has been cleansed and softened, manual extraction of comedones can be performed. The esthetician will put on gloves and wrap their fingers in cotton or gauze. A small amount of astringent should be applied to the tips of the fingers. To effectively remove a comedone, the esthetician will use the sides of their fingers to apply firm pressure to the skin surrounding it. It may be necessary to apply pressure from different angles to fully remove the comedone from the follicle. Some comedones can be removed by applying downward pressure with the finger, then pushing upward from underneath the comedone. Once a comedone has been extracted, it should be placed on a tissue for disposal. Extractions should begin at the chin, then move to the nose, cheeks, forehead, and upper cheek bones. It is necessary to remove and dispose of gloves used during extractions before providing other facial services to prevent spread of bacteria.

Estheticians may choose to use the following tools when extracting comedones as an alternative to manual removal with the fingers:

- **Cotton Swabs**: The esthetician holds cotton swabs between their index finger and thumb. They are used to apply pressure to the skin surrounding comedones, similar to the pressure used when extracting with the fingers.
- **Comedone Extractor**: Comedone extractors are metal tools that have loops on each end, one that is small and one that is slightly larger. The loop is placed over the comedone and pressed gently around it. Upward and outward pressure is used to remove the blemish.
- **Lancet**: The use of a lancet is not permissible in all states, so the esthetician should ensure they are permitted to use one before offering treatment. The lancet is held at a 35-degree angle and used to pierce the skin horizontally releasing the trapped sebum. Downward pressure is then applied around the pierced area to remove the debris from the follicle. Lancets should be disposed of in a sharps container.

Functions and Applications of Masks

Facial masks are any treatment applied to and allowed to sit on the skin of the face. Facial masks range in purpose and benefit. Estheticians will select a mask treatment based on the client's skin type and goals. Some masks are gentle, moisturizing, and nourishing while others are formulated with harsher ingredients and meant for oily, acne prone skin or to treat signs of aging. The most common benefits of masking are a brighter, healthier looking complexion, nourished skin, and clean pores. Masks used in salon settings typically contain ingredients at strengths only available to a licensed esthetician. To continue treatments at home, a variety of masks can be purchased and used independently by clients. While there are several masks to address a multitude of concerns, they can all be classified as either setting or non-setting masks. Setting masks dry and harden when applied to the skin while non-setting masks stay moist.

Non-setting masks are characterized by their ability to remain moist. Unlike setting masks, these do not dry or harden on the skin. Most non-setting masks contain plant-based ingredients meant to soothe and provide moisture. Gel and cream masks are the most common examples. Non-setting masks are typically used for moisturizing treatments and are most beneficial to sensitive, inflamed, irritated, aging, dry, or dehydrated skin. These masks are applied to the face and allowed to sit so that the ingredients may penetrate and treat the skin. At the end of non-setting mask treatments, the mask is either wiped away or any remaining liquid is massaged into the skin and acts as a serum. Sheet masks are another popular example of non-setting masks. They may come premoistened or freeze-dried. Freeze-dried masks are moistened after they are applied to the skin.

Setting masks dry and harden after they are applied to the skin. There are four types of setting masks:

- **Clay masks**: Used to draw out oil and impurities. They also stimulate circulation and cause the pores to contract.
- **Alginate**: Seaweed based masks that come in a powdered form that are dehydrated and applied to the skin following a serum or treatment. They form a seal on the skin that encourages absorption of the treatment that was applied prior.
- **Modelage masks**: Also known as thermal masks, these often come in a powder form which are then mixed with water and applied to the face in layers over gauze. This raises the temperature of the skin to promote circulation and penetration of active ingredients.
- **Paraffin wax masks**: Wax heated to just above body temperature is applied to the skin over nourishing creams. It promotes circulation and absorption of the cream that was applied previously.

After selecting a mask that is appropriate for the client, the esthetician will remove the mask from its container and place it in either a small bowl or the palm of their hand before applying it with a brush or spatula. Starting at the neck, long and slow strokes are used to evenly apply the mask. When applying the mask to the face, strokes should begin at the center of the face and move outward. The eye area should be avoided, as it is too delicate for most masks. Once the mask has been allowed to sit and harden, typically 7-10 minutes, it may be removed. For clay masks, an esthetician should use warm, moistened towels, whereas alginate and wax masks are typically formulated to be peeled from the skin. Modelage masks can be removed by using gentle pressure to lift the hardened mask from the face. Once the mask has been removed, toner, serum, and moisturizer are applied.

Sheet masks are a type of non-setting mask and have a unique application process. Before using a sheet mask, a serum may be applied to the skin if desired. Wearing gloves, the esthetician will open the packet and remove the mask. Some sheet masks have a backing that will need to be removed when applying. Application begins at the chin and continues upward by smoothing the mask over the skin and positioning it to ensure all areas are covered. If the sheet mask being used is freeze-dried, water will need to be applied to the mask after it is positioned on the face to activate the ingredients. Pre-moistened masks are applied directly to the skin without adding water. The mask should sit on the skin according to the manufacturer instructions before it is removed. Removal begins at the chin where the mask is lifted and peeled upward. Depending on the ingredients in the mask and manufacturer instructions, the liquid left on the skin may be massaged into the skin or wiped away.

Cotton compresses are used to aid in removal of setting face masks. These are also referred to as cotton mummy masks. The warmth and moisture of the cotton cloths used help to continue soothing and calming the skin during mask removal, and use of disposable cloths helps maintain a sanitary workspace. When it is time to remove the mask, a 4" x 4" cloth should be opened to 4" x 8" and saturated with warm water. After ringing out the excess moisture, the first piece of cotton will be used to cover the neck before being repeated to cover the chin and mouth. It may be necessary to create a hole in the cloth for the mouth. Another saturated cloth will be placed across the bridge of the nose and the eyes, taking care not to block the nostrils. A final cloth is applied to the forehead. Removal starts at the forehead with the esthetician using a flat hand to wipe the product away with the top cloth. That cloth is removed, and the process is repeated until no cloth or product remains on the face.

Conclusion of Facial Services

Following treatment, clients should be asked how they are feeling and if they enjoyed their services. Providers should listen receptively and take this time to explain what they noticed about the area of treatment and what results could be achieved with continued treatment. If the client is interested, they can work together to determine a plan for future visits. The provider needs to explain what care should be taken at home to support and prolong the treatment that was provided. This is also an opportunity for the provider to promote products they have available for retail. The client should be escorted to the reception desk where the provider will complete a service ticket that outlines what treatment was provided, what home care was recommended, and when another appointment should take place. The provider should then review the ticket with the client and schedule their next appointment if desired. After the transaction is complete, the provider should record service information.

Use of Electrical Equipment Used in Skin Services

Electrotherapy is the use of electric devices to treat the skin. While electrical devices are not necessary to perform facials, they do produce more visible changes in the client's complexion. The majority of these devices are used to aid skin analysis, help products to penetrate the skin, or provide exfoliating treatments. Because there are several different devices that fall into this category, an esthetician must familiarize themselves with each machine they use and adhere to the manufacturer guidelines for each specific tool. Hot towel cabinets and magnifying lamps are common and less advanced examples of electrotherapy devices. More intense electrotherapy tools include galvanic current machines, high frequency machines, and vacuum machines. Most intense electrotherapy devices should not be used on clients who:

- Have heart conditions or a pacemaker
- Are pregnant
- Have a seizure disorder
- Have broken skin
- Are fearful of electric current

A hot towel cabinet, also referred to as a towel warmer or hot cabbie, is used in treatment rooms to heat towels or products that will be applied to the skin. Hot towels are used to remove facial masks and products and to soften the skin before extractions are performed. They should not be used on clients with sensitive skin, skin disorders, or broken skin. Due to risk of burns, the temperature of towels and heated products should be tested before application to a client's skin. The esthetician can do this by holding the towel or applying a small amount of the product to their wrist to assess how warm it is. Maintaining a hot towel cabinet requires it to be cleaned inside and out with an EPA registered disinfectant at the end of each day. It should be left open overnight so that it may fully dry. Trays underneath the cabinet should be drained and disinfected daily. To help prevent bacteria from entering the cabinet, the esthetician should ensure they are using clean gloves to remove towels.

A magnifying **lamp** allows estheticians to examine their client's skin more closely than they could with their naked eye by using magnifying lenses and fluorescent lighting directly over the client. These lamps are used during skin analysis, during extractions, and any time more lighting is needed throughout treatment. Due to the intensity of the light used in these lamps, it is necessary for the client's eyes to be covered before the lamp is positioned over them and while it is in use. The adjustable nature and frequent repositioning of magnifying lamps make them prone to damage. Investing in a high-quality magnifying lamp, adjusting the lamp carefully, and performing regular maintenance increases the longevity of the lamp. The esthetician should regularly check for and tighten loose screws and hinges. The lenses on these lamps should be cleaned with disinfectant and a soft cloth, as using a paper towel or tissue will scratch and damage the lens. The entirety of the lamp should be disinfected after each use.

Wood's lamps use filtered black light to illuminate fungi, bacterial disorders, pigmentation problems, and similar skin issues that are not visible to the naked eye during skin analysis. Different skin conditions are characterized by different colored appearances under the lamp:

- **Thick skin**: white fluorescence
- **Dead skin cells**: white spots
- **Normal, healthy skin**: blue-white
- **Think or dehydrated skin**: Purple, light purple
- **Acne or bacteria**: yellow or orange
- **Oily skin or comedones**: Yellow, pink, or orange
- **Hyperpigmentation or sun damage**: brown
- **Hypopigmentation**: blue-white or yellow green

This allows the esthetician to gain better insight into the quality of the client's skin and to treat conditions they may have otherwise missed. Wood's lamps must be used in completely dark treatment rooms to be used effectively, should be disinfected according to manufacturer instructions after each use, and should be stored in a safe place to protect the bulb.

Rotary brushes, also referred to as facial brushes, are used to manually exfoliate the skin. They come in a variety of sizes with settings that allow for variance in the speed and direction of the brush. As with all forms of exfoliation, precautions must be taken. Rotary brushes should not be used on sensitive, irritated, inflamed, or broken skin. Gentle pressure should be used to pass the moistened brush over the skin in a manner that is tolerable to each client's skin type. Oily and acne prone skin can tolerate faster movement while dry skin requires slower movement. To maintain rotary brushes, the attachments must first be removed and washed with soap and water. They can then be soaked in disinfectant. The handpiece cannot be soaked due to the electrical components. They should be wiped with a disinfectant according to the manufacturer's instructions. All pieces should be allowed to dry thoroughly before storing so that the bristles on the brush heads are not damaged.

A vacuum machine is also referred to as a suction machine. It is most commonly used to remove dirt and impurities from the skin, stimulate the dermal layer of the skin, and aid in lymphatic drainage. The suction cups used on vacuum machines are made of either glass or metal and come in a variety of shapes and sizes to accommodate use on different areas of the face, neck, and chest. During facials, vacuum machines are used after desincrustation but before extractions. They may also be used in place of facial massage. Vacuum machines should not be used on red or inflamed skin or skin with open lesions. Using too much pressure when suctioning the skin can cause bruising or tissue damage. Glass and metal attachments should be cleaned with soap and water, then disinfected. Hand pieces should be cleaned according to manufacturer instructions. Most vacuum machines have filters located at the end of the hose that require frequent changing.

Galvanic machines convert alternating electrical current received from an electrical outlet into a direct current. These electrons in the current flow continuously in one direction and can be targeted to specific nerve endings in the epidermis. This creates a relaxation response in the nerve endings. Galvanic currents create two reactions used in esthetic treatments, desincrustation and ionic iontophoresis. Desincrustation prepares the skin for extractions. Ionic iontophoresis helps deliver products to the skin more effectively. Galvanic machines should not be used on clients with:

- Pacemakers, metal implants, or braces
- Heart conditions
- Epilepsy
- Pregnancy
- High blood pressure
- Open, broken, inflamed, irritated, or sensitive skin
- Migraine headaches
- Any sign on illness or infection

After use, electrodes should be disconnected from their cords and any cotton on the electrode should be removed before it is washed and disinfected. The remainder of the equipment should be cleaned and disinfected per manufacturer instructions.

Desincrustation is accomplished through a chemical reaction between galvanic currents and the skin in which sebum and debris are emulsified. This treatment is beneficial for oily, acne prone skin. To begin desincrustation, the esthetician applies an alkaline solution to the skin. The solution sits on top of the skin and is not absorbed. The client will hold the positive electrode from the galvanic machine while the esthetician uses the negative electrode to contact the face. A chemical reaction called saponification occurs in which salt in the skin's sebum converts to sodium hydroxide. This creates a soap like substance that dissolves excess oil and clears debris from follicles. When using a galvanic machine for desincrustation, it is important that the esthetician maintains contact between the electrode and the client's face to prevent shocking them. The electrode should not be removed until the current has been shut off.

Iontophoresis uses electricity from a galvanic machine to introduce water-soluble solutions to the skin. This allows the ions of the solutions to transfer into deeper layers of the skin, far beyond the skin's barrier. Both positive and negative currents from the galvanic machine flow through conductive solution applied to the skin. The currents separate the solution into ions by their polarity, either positive or negative, in a process known as ionization. Positively charged ions penetrate the skin in a process called cataphoresis. Cataphoresis causes an acidic reaction with the solution, tightens the skin, calms nerve endings, and decreases blood circulation. Anaphoresis is the process in which negatively charged ions enter the skin. Anaphoresis causes an alkaline reaction with the skin, softens skin tissue, stimulates

84

nerve endings, and increases blood flow. Together, these processes help improve the texture and appearance of skin.

High-frequency machines use **sinusoidal current**, an alternating current, to vibrate water molecules into the skin and produce heat. To use a high-frequency machine, an electrode tip is selected based on the service and attached to the handpiece. Once the electrode contacts the skin, it can be used for a few purposes, such as creating ozone that acts as an antiseptic on the skin. This helps prevent the growth and spread of bacteria, which is especially beneficial after extractions. The heat generated during treatment helps products penetrate the skin. High-frequency machines also stimulate circulation, increase cell metabolism, and help oxygenate the skin. These machines should not be used on clients with:

- Inflamed or irritated skin
- Heart problems, pacemakers, or high blood pressure
- Metal implants or braces
- Medical conditions like pregnancy or epilepsy
- Body piercings above the waist

Special care should be taken to ensure a client does not contact metal in any form during treatment, as it can lead to burns. After each use, electrodes should be cleaned with soap and water. The handpiece, cords, and machine should be cleaned with disinfectant. These machines require regular maintenance that can be found in manufacturer guidelines.

Electrodes are the glass tips used on high-frequency machines. Air is removed from the electrodes and replaced with neon, argon, or rarefied gas during manufacturing. Electricity passes through the gas in the electrodes causing visible light to emit in varying shades. When selecting an electrode, an esthetician must consider the skin type of the client and the condition that they will be treating. The pink, orange, or red gas from neon gas is best for aging or sensitive skin, while the blue or violet light from argon or rarefied gas is used for normal, oily, or acne prone skin. Electrodes used in high-frequency treatment vary in shape and size. The most commonly seen electrodes are:

- Small mushroom
- Large mushroom
- Indirect
- Sparking
- Comb

Electrodes should be gently cleansed after each use. They should never be submerged or cleaned with harsh chemicals. Electrodes are very fragile and should be handled and stored with care.

Spray machines are vacuum machine attachments. They consist of a bottle with a spray nozzle that is attached to the machine by a hose. They are filled with toner solution which is gently misted onto a client's face after cleansing or whenever moisture needs to be added to hydrate the skin. Spray machines should not be used on clients with respiratory issues as they can cause further irritation and interfere with breathing. They also should not be used in rooms that are not well ventilated as they produce fumes from the toning solution. Solutions left in spray machines can cause the bottle to degrade over time. As such, the bottles should be emptied and cleaned on a regular basis. Spray nozzles should also be cleaned regularly to prevent mineral buildup. Flushing the machine regularly will help to prevent buildup throughout the machine. As with all machines used in skin treatments, the exterior portion of a spray machine should be disinfected after use.

Makeup

PRINCIPLES

Makeup consultations should begin with the client completing a questionnaire on which they answer several makeup-related questions. Common questions include their needs and expectations, if the makeup is for a special occasion, what level of makeup they would feel comfortable wearing, any concerns or areas on which they would like to focus, and preferred colors to use in the look. For safety reasons, it is also important to ask if the client has any known allergies, wears contacts, has sensitive skin, or is currently taking, or has recently taken, medication used to treat conditions of the skin. Once the client has completed the questionnaire, the esthetician should review it with them to ensure the information is correct and address any outstanding questions. The esthetician or client may want to use pictures of similar looks when explaining the desired outcome to ensure both parties have the same expectations. The esthetician may proceed with the makeup application following the consultation.

Color theory is the science surrounding use of color in art and other visual mediums. In cosmetics it is the basis for selecting makeup colors. To best utilize color theory, it is important that estheticians understand the color wheel. The **color wheel** is a visual representation of colors based on the three **primary colors**—blue, red, and yellow. **Secondary colors**, orange, green, and purple, are made by mixing equal parts of primary colors. **Tertiary colors** are created by mixing equal amounts of a neighboring primary and secondary color. Red-orange and blue-green are two of many examples. Using the color wheel, estheticians can find complementary and analogous colors to use in makeup application. **Complementary colors** are those across from one another on the color wheel. Using complementary colors for eyeshadow helps to create a more flattering, dynamic look, such as using orange-based colors on clients with blue eyes. **Analogous colors**, those that are side by side, are used to create softer looks.

The first step in selecting an appropriate foundation color is to determine the client's skin tone. **Tone** is typically classified as light, medium, or dark, and is also known as hue. The esthetician must then determine the undertone. The **undertone** is the subtle warm or cool appearance beneath the skin. It will fall into one of three categories:

- **Cool**: Pink, red, or bluish undertones
- **Warm**: Yellow, peach, or golden undertones
- **Neutral**: Mix of cool and warm undertones

Using a foundation with an incorrect undertone will not allow for a seamless blend between the product and the client's skin. Some skin conditions will require use of foundations with tinted bases regardless of a client's undertones. Green based foundations can be used to cancel out red, ruddy skin while pink based foundations can be used to conceal yellow, sallow skin. After establishing the tone and undertone, a properly matching foundation can be selected.

When selecting an eyeshadow color, an esthetician has three options. Using neutral tone eyeshadow is a safe option for all clients as they complement all eye, skin, and hair colors. Eyeshadow that is the same color as the client's eyes will create a monochromatic look with minimal depth or visual contrast, whereas using complementary colors will create a more flattering look. The three basic eye colors and their complementary eyeshadow colors are:

- **Blue eyes**: Shadows with any shades of orange or the primary colors that create orange (red and yellow). Popular options include all shades of brown and neutrals, gold, copper, peach, and mauve.
- **Green eyes**: Red is the complementary color of green; however, it should not be used as it creates an appearance of fatigue or illness in the client. Brown-based reds, rust, copper, pink, plum, and purple are acceptable options.
- **Brown eyes**: Brown eyes are neutral and are enhanced by any color. Blue is complementary to brown, making it an acceptable choice along with greens, grays, and silvers.

PRODUCT SELECTION

Foundation is used to even out the color and texture of the skin and protect the skin from environmental factors. It is sometimes referred to as base makeup. It is created by combining pigments, emollients, and humectants with bases that are applied to the skin. There are four common bases:

- **Oil based**: Formulated using mineral oil, good for normal to dry skin.
- **Water based**: Used to achieve a matte finish, good for oily and sensitive skin.
- **Silicone based**: Longer lasting, occludes pores to create an even surface.
- **Alcohol based**: Extremely durable and transfer resistant, used primarily in special effects makeup.

Some foundations may contain additional ingredients to benefit the skin such as sunscreen, vitamins, or acne treatments. A foundation made for daily use will typically either be a liquid or cream formulation. Cake makeup and greasepaint are much heavier formulations and are commonly reserved for theater use. To extend the wear of foundation, a primer may be used before application. Primers adhere to the skin and create a smooth surface for the foundation to stick to.

Use of concealer, face powder, blush, and highlighter:

- **Concealer**: Used to cover blemishes in a manner that is heavier and more targeted than foundation. It is applied directly to and around a blemish and comes in several formats including wands, sticks, pots, and pencils. Concealers containing additional ingredients to treat the skin, such as those with acne medication or moisturizers, are available.
- **Face powder**: Used to mattify (remove shine) the face or set foundation. Comes in loose and pressed formats. Available in all skin tones as well as unpigmented. Face powders vary in weight and coverage, and application method.
- **Blush**: Pigment applied to the cheeks to enhance skin tone. It is usually a pink or red based product. Available in powder, cream, gel, and liquid formulations and is applied after foundation to create a more natural appearance.
- **Highlighter**: Pigment that is lighter than the client's skin tone and is used to accentuate the highpoints of a client's facial bone structure. Most often used under the eyebrow, at the temples, on the chin, and on the cheek bones. Available in liquid, powder, and cream formulations.

Types of commonly used cosmetics for eyes:

- **Eyeshadow**: Used to accentuate and reshape the eyes. Available in a variety of colors and finishes, such as matte or shimmer. Available in loose or pressed powder, cream, stick, and liquid formulations.
- **Eyeliner**: Used to emphasize or reshape the eyes. Available in a variety of colors with neutrals such as black, brown, or gray being most common for daily wear. Available in pencil, liquid, pressed, or gel formulations.
- **Eyebrow color**: Used to correct the shape of or darken the eyebrows. Available in a variety of shades to match the color of natural eyebrows. Available in pencil, powder, pomade, and gel formulations.
- **Mascara**: Used to define, lengthen, thicken, and darken the eyelashes. Available in a variety of colors with black and brown being the most popular. Available in liquid, cake, and cream form. Mascara is also available in a regular formulation that is easy to remove with regular remover and waterproof formulations that are designed to stay intact when contacting moisture.

Types of commonly used cosmetics for lips:

- **Lip color**: Used to enhance or give color to the face or to make a look appear finished. These are available in a variety of colors and most commonly come in cream, gloss, pencil and stick formulations. Lip stains are a lip color option that is growing in popularity. Some lip color products contain SPF to protect the lips from the sun and act as moisturizers to hydrate the lips.
- **Lip gloss**: Used to provide a sheen to the lips. Glosses may or may not be tinted. Plumping glosses cause a reaction with the skin through use of a mild irritant that expands blood vessels and causes increased blood flow in the lips, creating a plumper appearance.
- **Lip liner**: Used to create a border that keeps lipstick from spreading from the lips or to fill in uneven areas around the lip. Most often found in pencil formulations and available in a variety of colors to match lip color products.
- **Lip conditioner**: Used to hydrate and condition the lips before applying lip color products.

An esthetician should have a well-stocked cosmetic kit that is designed based on the needs and desires of their clients. The most commonly used supplies in a cosmetics kit are:

- **Sponges**: used for blending
- **Spatulas**: used for removing products from containers
- **Tissues**: used for blotting
- **Wand**: used for applying mascara
- **Brow comb**: used to brush and position eyebrows
- **Lash comb**: used to separate eyelashes
- **Cotton swabs**: used for application and cleaning of eye makeup
- **Paper drapes**: used to protect the client's clothing
- **Cleaning agents**: used to clean brushes between uses
- **Brushes**: used to apply powder makeup products
- **Cape**: used to cover a client's clothing
- **Tweezers**: used to remove stray hairs
- **Sharpeners**: used to sharpen pencils used in makeup, such as eyeliner and lipliner
- **Mirror**: used for client to view makeup application
- **Mixing cups**: used for blending and mixing foundation
- **Lash curler**: used to curl lashes before applying mascara
- **Hair clips or headbands**: used to hold the client's hair away from their face

Makeup brushes come in a variety of shapes and sizes depending on their use. All brushes are composed of three parts: the hair, handle, and ferrule. The hair is also known as the bristles and is the part of the brush used to apply makeup to the skin. The handle is the portion of the brush the esthetician holds with their hand. The ferrule is the metal portion that is clamped to affix the hair to the handle. The most commonly used brushes are:

- **Powder brushes**: Large, soft bristles
- **Blush brush**: Smaller, tapered version of a powder brush
- **Foundation brush**: Long, flat bristles with rounded end
- **Concealer brush**: Short, flat, densely packed bristles
- **Kabuki brush**: Short, wide, densely packed bristles
- **Eyeshadow brush**: Range in size and texture depending on use
- **Eyeliner brush**: Small, firm, tapered bristles
- **Angled brow brush**: Firm, thing, angled bristles
- **Lash and brow brush**: Double sided. The comb on one side is used for the lashes while the short bristles on the other side brush the eyebrows
- **Lip brush**: Small, tapered bristles with a rounded edge

APPLICATION

Understanding face shapes allows an esthetician to appropriately accentuate and de-emphasize their clients' facial features during makeup application. Sharing information about face shapes with a client also empowers them to make decisions regarding flattering hairstyles, glasses, and other accessories. There are seven face shapes.

- **Oval**: The face is widest at the temple and forehead and tapers to a curved chin. Oval faces are considered the ideal face shape due to their symmetry.
- **Round**: The face is widest at the cheekbones with round jawline and soft chin. It is usually the same length as it is width.
- **Square**: The face has a wide jawline and forehead.
- **Rectangle**: Also known as oblong. The face is long and narrow, often with hollow cheeks.
- **Triangle**: Also known as pear-shaped. The face is widest at the jaw line and tapers upward.
- **Heart**: The face is widest at the temple and forehead and tapers to a narrow chin.
- **Diamond**: The face is widest at the cheekbones and has a narrow forehead and chin.

When appropriately applied, foundation smooths the appearance of the skin and creates an even base for the rest of the makeup to be applied to. Prior to a makeup appointment, clients should exfoliate and moisturize their skin to ensure smooth application. The esthetician may choose to apply a primer before application to give the foundation something to adhere to and to allow the makeup to last longer. Foundation can be applied with a brush or disposable sponge. Sponges may be used when wet or dry. A thin, even layer of foundation should be applied to the skin and blended up to the hairline, down the jaw, and along the edges of the face. Gentle pressure should be used to apply and blend the foundation, taking special care around the eyes. Stippling, a patting motion used to spread foundation across the skin, provides better coverage than rubbing. It can be used to evenly build coverage where needed.

Concealer can be applied before or after foundation and is typically used below the eyes and to cover blemishes. Concealers are available in a variety of shades and tones that are meant to correct different skin flaws. In most cases, concealers should match as closely to the foundation used as possible, as using a concealer that is too light or too dark will draw more attention to the area being covered. A small amount of concealer should be applied to the problem area, then blended into the surrounding skin. Color correcting concealers are tinted with non-skin-colored pigments. Green and yellow based concealers cover red toned areas, purple-based concealers brighten the skin, and peach, red, and pink concealers cover dark areas. Concealers may also be used for highlighting and contouring. Using a concealer lighter than the client's skin will accentuate the area to which it has been applied, whereas using a darker concealer will make the area less visually pronounced.

Highlighting and contouring are used together to accentuate the face by making highpoints more prominent and minimizing other areas. **Highlighters** are a shade of makeup that is lighter than a client's foundation and are often applied to the brow bone, temples, chin, and cheekbones to bring out these features. **Contour** shades are darker than the client's foundation and are applied anywhere the client wants their features to appear smaller, typically below the cheek bones and along the sides of the nose. These products come in liquid and powder forms and are usually applied using a brush or sponge.

Blush is used to accentuate cheekbones and give the face additional color after applying foundation. It is typically a red or pink tone that is applied just below the cheekbones and blended upward towards the temples, but it should not touch the hairline. Blush comes in powder, liquid, and cream formulations and is applied using a sponge or brush.

Face powder should match the tone of the foundation used or should be translucent (colorless) to ensure a seamless blend. It is used to set foundation and concealer. Powder is applied in circular, downward motions using a large, soft brush. Powder products come in loose and pressed formats. Loose powders come in jars, making them ideal for estheticians to use hygienically. A small amount of powder is deposited onto a clean makeup palette to be used on the client. A brush is swirled through the powder, the excess is tapped off, and the powder remaining on the brush is applied. Pressed powder comes in a compact, making it easier to carry but less than ideal for estheticians to use. Pressed powders can be made loose for application by scraping the product with a spatula or disinfected brush onto a clean makeup palette. If too much powder has been applied to a client, it can be removed using a damp sponge or by spritzing the face with water.

Eye makeup typically consists of eyeshadow, eyeliner, mascara, and brow color.

- **Eyeshadow**: Before applying eyeshadow, an eyelid primer may be used to give the eyeshadow a base on which to adhere. A base color is applied first across the entire eye from brow to bone. A contour color is darker than the client's skin tone and is used in the crease or on the lash line. A highlight color is lighter than the client's skin tone and used to accentuate an area. Eyeshadow is applied with a brush using a soft, sweeping motion.
- **Eyeliner**: Eyeliner is used to shape the eye. It can be applied before or after eyeshadow and is used along the lash line. It should be applied using gentle, short strokes.
- **Mascara**: Mascara is used to accentuate the eyelashes. It should be applied to the upper and lower lashes using a single-use wand using a side-to-side motion. Lashes can be curled before application for more emphasis.
- **Brows**: The eyebrow color used should complement the color of the client's hair. It is applied to the brows using a sweeping motion and blended inside the brow line.

Lip colors come in a variety of shades and formulas. An esthetician should consider the overall makeup design and client preference when selecting a lip product. Light colors are used to make lips appear larger while dark colors minimize the lip's appearance. Lip conditioners can be used to prep lips for applying lip color. They should be applied at the beginning of the makeup session to allow them to set. Lip liner can be applied to define and shape the lips before applying an all over lip color. Liner colors should match the lip color as closely as possible. Lip color and glosses should be applied with either single-use applicators or single-use brushes using even strokes to ensure the color is contained within the borders of the lips. Lip liner, lipstick, and lip gloss can be applied in that order for the longest-lasting, most finished look.

Proper and safe application begins with a prepared esthetician. Fingernails should be kept short and smooth to avoid scratching clients and hands should be thoroughly washed before makeup application begins. An esthetician should keep a stock of single-use and disposable tools in their kit along with a brush disinfectant solution to prevent the spread of bacteria between clients. Makeup should be applied with a light touch, and tugging and pulling the skin should be avoided. Extra care should be taken when applying makeup around the eye as the skin in that area is thin and delicate. Cream and liquid makeup should be applied before powder as applying in reverse order does not allow the makeup to blend. Foundation and powder should be applied downward in the direction of hair growth for a smoother finish. Proper bracing techniques should be used throughout makeup application to avoid both hurting the client and smudging makeup.

Highlighting and contouring can minimize or accentuate facial features:

- **Round or square face**: Blend a dark shade on the outer edges and temples and apply a lighter shade from the center of the forehead down the center of the face.
- **Triangular face**: Apply a dark shade to the chin and neck and a light shade under the eyes and on the cheeks. Blend together for a natural finish.
- **Narrow face**: Blend a lighter shade to the cheek bones and outer edges of the face.
- **Wide jaw**: Use a darker shade below the cheekbones and along the jawline before blending downward into the neck.
- **Double chin**: Blend a darker shade under the jawline and on the chin.
- **Long, prominent chin**: Apply darker foundation to the chin and blend.
- **Receding chin**: Apply lighter foundation to the chin and blend.
- **Protruding forehead**: Apply a darker shade of foundation to the forehead.
- **Narrow forehead**: Apply lighter foundation along the hairline and blend to the forehead.
- **Wide nose**: Apply a darker shade to the sides of the nose and a lighter shade down the middle. Blend them together.
- **Short nose**: Blend a lighter shade on the tip of the nose and between the eyes.

Eyeshadow colors can be used to reshape the eyes and enhance the overall appearance of a client. The method of application used will depend on the shape and size of the eyes.

- **Monolids**: Use a dark shadow to create a crease in the middle of the lid, highlight the brow bone, thinly line the eyes, and apply brown mascara.
- **Small eyes**: Use a light shadow across the lid, use a darker color to crease the outer corner, apply liner lightly or skip, apply mascara.
- **Round eyes**: Use a medium shadow over the entire eyelid, apply a dark shadow to the crease and blend outward, apply eyeliner and mascara, applying more mascara to the outer corner of the lashes.
- **Protruding eyelids**: Use a medium shadow to coat the entire lid, apply a dark shadow to the prominent part of the lid, highlight the brow bone, line the eye and apply mascara.

The way that eyes are set will determine the most flattering eye makeup application process.

- **Deep-set eyes**: Use a light, reflective shadow across the lid and blend a medium color next to the outer corner, line the eyes and apply a dark mascara.
- **Close-set eyes**: Use a pale shadow across the lid with a darker one in the outer corner, line the eye from the middle outward and apply mascara.

- **Wide-set eyes**: Use a darker shadow on the inner corner of the eye and blend a lighter shadow from the middle outward, apply liner all the way to the inner edge of the eye and apply mascara.
- **Downward sloping eyes**: Use a medium color shadow across the fold of the eye and upward, apply highlighter under the arch of the brow, apply a thin line of eyeliner or skip eyeliner, and apply mascara.

A variety of lip colors and techniques can be used to reshape the lips and make them appear better proportioned. For small or thin lips and mouths, a lip liner can be used to draw an extension of the lips by following the natural shape of the lips just above or below the actual lips. The border and lips are filled in with lip color. A similar technique can be used to reshape asymmetrical, downturned, or straight lips. The lips are lined with a more ideal shape, then filled in with color. For large, full lips, a thin line should be drawn just inside the lip line and a soft, flat lip color should be applied. For pointed upper lips, liner can be used to curve and round out the natural points of the lips before filling in with a lip color.

Clients seek specialty makeup looks from estheticians for a variety of occasions. Brides will be the center of attention and highly photographed on their wedding day, making bridal makeup services a key part of the preparation process for the wedding. These services are typically booked months in advance, and a trial is performed to ensure the bride will be satisfied with their look. The esthetician should be involved in creating a timeline to ensure makeup services stay on track. Clients may also seek makeup services for other events that will be photographed or videoed. Due to the impact of high-definition cameras on the look of makeup, it is necessary to use more intense colors on the eyes, lips, and cheeks so that they stand out visually on camera. There are high-definition makeup products available that appear more natural on camera than other daily use products. Some clients may seek camouflage makeup to cover tattoos, scarring, or postoperative healing. This type of makeup requires more intensive training than the aforementioned methods.

Permanent makeup is similar to tattooing, as it also deposits pigment into the upper layer of the dermis. Most states require additional licensure to practice permanent makeup application in addition to being a licensed esthetician. Traditional tattoo machines, pens, or rotary machines are used to apply permanent makeup. While it is referred to as permanent makeup, the ink can fade over time and may require touch ups. Eyeliner and eyebrow application are the most popular forms of permanent makeup. Microblading is another permanent makeup treatment growing in popularity that uses small needles on a handpiece to insert pigment into the skin of the eyebrows, creating a fuller and more sculpted look. Lip color, scar camouflage, and body art are less popular forms of permanent makeup. Mild swelling and inflammation are common after permanent makeup application and may last up to 72 hours. The colors applied will appear much darker for the first six-to-ten days before beginning to lighten to a more natural color.

SAFETY

Bracing is a technique used to protect clients from injuries and prevent makeup from smudging and transferring during application. It requires the esthetician to position their hands and keep them steady in a way that minimizes the amount of pressure applied to the client's face, but still allows the esthetician to support their hands and wrists. It is most commonly utilized during eye makeup applications. The esthetician will place the back of their dominant hand on the client's face, just above the brow, while using the fingers of that hand to move makeup brushes and applicators. They may elect to place a tissue or clean powder puff between their hand and the client's skin to prevent transfer of makeup. Some estheticians will use their nondominant hand to hold their opposite wrist steady. Bracing may also be used when applying lip color to help ensure liner is applied in an even, controlled manner and lipstick does not go beyond the border created by the liner.

INFECTION CONTROL

As with all other esthetic procedures, estheticians should wash their hands before beginning any makeup services. Products should not be removed from their containers with fingers or hands as this can spread bacteria. Clean spatulas should be used for removal. Pressed powders can be scraped with a spatula onto a clean palette, while loose powders can be dispensed from their jar onto the palette. Products that come in tubes, such as lip and brow colors, can be removed with a spatula and applied to the palette, or they may be removed with a single-use applicator and applied directly to the client. Single-use applicators should be disposed of immediately after use and not dipped back into the product. Products that can be sharpened, like eye and lip liners encased in wood, may be used directly on the client and then sharpened with a disinfected sharpener to remove any portion that contacted a client's skin. If a product becomes contaminated, it should be disposed of or may be given to the client.

Many estheticians prefer to use makeup brushes instead of disposable applicators because they often provide better, more precise coverage. To safely use these brushes on multiple clients and minimize the spread of bacteria, brushes must be cleaned and disinfected between clients. There are two options for cleaning makeup brushes. When using them in a setting where quick cleaning is required, such as providing makeup services to a group of clients, an alcohol-based cleaner can be used to quickly clean and sanitize the brush. However, alcohol cleaners should be used sparingly as they dry out and damage brush bristles. If time allows, it is better to wash brushes with a gentle soap or cleanser made for makeup brushes, then rinse with warm water to remove the product. Brushes should be cleaned pointing downward and dried lying flat so that water does not seep into and damage the ferrule. After washing, brushes should be disinfected following the manufacturer instructions using an EPA registered disinfectant. It is important to note that natural bristles and wooden handles cannot be disinfected due to their porous nature and should not be used on clients.

Other Services

FACIAL SERVICES

Express facials are shortened facial services that take 15-to-30 minutes and omit some steps of a traditional facial. They are also referred to as mini-facials. Express facials begin in the same manner as regular facials with a consultation and draping the client. For some express facial services, clients may opt to leave on their eye makeup. Cleansing and masking are the most important steps in an express facial, and steaming, massage, and extractions are often omitted. Other treatment options for express facials include focusing on one area of the face, such as the t-zone, or application of more intense treatments for exfoliation or hydration. Express facials may be incorporated into other services, such as beard care, or performed alongside other short services like waxing or pedicures. Express facials should end with application of SPF and moisturizer, recommendation of products for use at home, and planning for a client's next visit.

Estheticians can play a vital role in pre- and postoperative treatments for patients. In both cases, the esthetician helps educate the client regarding what to expect and how to treat their skin at home before and after an operation. Preoperative care focuses on prepping the skin for operation. Making the skin as healthy as possible before surgery decreases recovery time and reduces damage to skin tissue. This can be achieved through peels, extractions, and exfoliation treatments. Postoperative care focuses on expediting wound healing and preventing infection. Massages, hydration treatment, and sun protection are the most important parts of postoperative care as they help decrease inflammation, soothe the skin, and protect the healing areas from sun damage. Permanent makeup and camouflage makeup can be used to cover scarring, tissue damage, or discoloration after surgery and may also be part of postoperative care provided by an esthetician.

Clinical procedures are those provided in a medical office or clinic setting that do not require surgery. Examples include injectables like fillers and Botox, laser treatments for hair and vein removal, and wrinkle treatment. Surgical procedures may be either reconstructive or cosmetic. Reconstructive surgery is performed to restore lost or impaired bodily functions. Patients receiving reconstructive surgery may have suffered trauma from an accident or may be seeking to treat a congenital disease or disfigurement. Cosmetic surgery is elective and does not impact the functions of the body. Examples of facial cosmetic surgery include rhytidectomy (face lift), blepharoplasty (eye lift), transconjunctival blepharoplasty (removal of fat pads under eyes), rhinoplasty (nose surgery), laser resurfacing, dermabrasion, and peels. Cosmetic surgery for the body includes sclerotherapy (varicose vein treatment), mammoplasty (breast reconstruction), liposuction, and abdominoplasty (fat removal). While estheticians cannot provide these treatments, they can assist a healthcare provider if they are trained and certified.

The most important role the esthetician can play in men's skincare is to educate them on their skincare needs, proper shaving techniques, and sun protection. Male clients tend to have skin that is sensitive and has suffered from years of mistreatment. They also have larger pores and more active sebaceous glands. This combination of sensitive, oily skin makes it necessary to provide both hydrating and deep cleansing treatments. Folliculitis and pseudofolliculitis are skin conditions commonly experienced by men. **Folliculitis** is inflammation of hair follicles, which can progress to **folliculitis barbae**, a bacterial infection caused by hair trapped under the follicle. **Pseudofolliculitis** appears as folliculitis, but without an infection. This is also known as razor burn. All of the aforementioned conditions can be prevented using proper shaving techniques and products that exfoliate and keep follicles clean. Inflammation and pustules can be treated by disinfecting the area. Most men will respond better to simple skincare routines and products that have more than one use, such as a moisturizer that can be used day or night.

Laser is an acronym for Light Amplification by Stimulated Emission of Radiation. These devices have numerous uses including hair removal and skin treatments. They work by emitting light into a chamber with mirrors that excite the light particles and cause them to gain energy. Once they gain enough energy, they can be used in treatment. Lasers are very precise and commonly used in noninvasive procedures. Different wavelengths of light are used to provide different treatments. For example, yellow light is absorbed by the skin and targets hemoglobin to destroy it without damaging normal skin cells. Lasers can be combined with radio frequencies to target connective tissue to produce a firming effect by stimulating collagen production. Other laser treatments include hair growth reduction, spider vein reduction, and skin peel promotion. Providing laser treatment requires extensive training and practice in addition to being a licensed esthetician.

Intense pulse light (IPL) devices use pulses to emit multiple wavelengths of light. The light is absorbed by hemoglobin to treat spider veins, melanin to treat discoloration, or hair follicles to remove unwanted hair. IPL can also be used to treat uneven skin, fine lines and wrinkles, and symptoms of rosacea. **Light-emitting diodes** (LEDs) use individual wavelengths of light in a variety of colors to address skin concerns. Red light is used to boost collagen production, stimulate wound healing, and speed up cell processes. Yellow light is used to reduce inflammation and improve lymphatic flow and circulation. Green light calms and soothes the skin to treat redness and hyperpigmentation. Blue lights reduce bacteria and help improve acne. No form of light therapy should be used on clients who have any form of photosensitivity, are pregnant, have cancer, or are taking antibiotics. It is important to cover the thyroid area during LED treatments as red-light LEDs are known to stimulate the thyroid.

Microcurrent devices deliver electrical currents that mimic the natural messages the brain sends to muscles. These treatments are also known as **wave therapy**. Wave therapy is used to treat conditions such as Bell's palsy and stroke paralysis in the medical field but has recently been introduced into the esthetics field to relax, tone, and strengthen muscles to combat signs of aging. Handheld probes are applied to the skin and moved following a technique that is dependent upon the application area. Visible results require weekly sessions for at least ten weeks followed by maintenance treatments every four weeks. Microcurrent may also be used to quicken the healing process. When used in conjunction with light therapy, microcurrent treatments have been found to be more effective. As with other electrical current devices, microcurrents should not be used on clients with conditions such as pregnancy, cancer, epilepsy, or any disease or disorder in the area to be treated. Any clients who receive injectable treatments such as filler should wait two weeks before receiving microcurrent treatments.

Ultrasound technology uses high frequency sound waves to penetrate the skin. This can stimulate tissue, increase blood flow, and promote oxygenation in addition to cleansing and exfoliating the skin. The lower the frequency of the waves, the deeper they penetrate. The heat and vibration created by ultrasound devices can be used to treat cellulite, as they promote drainage while stimulating circulation and cell metabolism. Ultrasound waves also allow products to deeply penetrate the skin through the process of sonophoresis. This technology is a good choice for providing exfoliation to clients with sensitive skin, as it is less abrasive than other chemical or manual exfoliants. Ultrasounds should not be used on clients with medical conditions such as cancer, diabetes, pregnancy, epilepsy, those who have pacemakers or other implants, or clients presenting with any visible skin disease or disorder. It is important to maintain contact with the skin and ensure the skin is moist throughout treatment to prevent excess heat buildup.

Microneedling, also known as dermal rolling, is a form of collagen induction therapy. A handpiece with a wheel of tiny needles is rolled across the skin. The needles prick the skin and cause the wound healing process to begin, which induces collagen and elastin formation. Because microneedling creates wounds, it has a one-to-three-day healing time and is considered a medical procedure in some states. It cannot be performed by estheticians in those states. **Nano infusion** is a popular treatment used where microneedling is not allowed. Nano infusion uses a handpiece similar to that used for microneedling, but it uses microscopic pyramid shaped modules made of silicone or surgical steel instead of needles. Instead of penetrating the dermis and causing wounds, nano tips create microchannels on top of the skin that assist penetration of skincare products into the skin. Nano infusion is less invasive than microneedling. Therefore, there is no associated recovery time.

Facial massages stimulate circulation and cell metabolism through rubbing, kneading, or otherwise manipulating the skin of the face. This leads to mental and physical benefits. Massage stimulates receptors in the nervous system that lead to overall feelings of relaxation. Studies have shown that massage lowers levels of the stress hormone cortisol in the body and increases levels of dopamine and serotonin, the neurotransmitters related to happiness. This leads to clients feeling happier and less stressed following a massage. Massage also helps to reduce muscle tension and relieve pain. The increased circulation and oxygenation provided by massage helps with transport of nutrients and removal of waste from cells. In addition, increased circulation and oxygenation assist in removal of dead skin cells and absorption of products. These benefits combine to promote cleaner, healthier, more evenly toned skin. Facial massages should not be given to clients who have inflamed, irritated, or otherwise sensitive skin, skin diseases or disorders, open sores or wounds, or uncontrolled hypertension or diabetes.

BODY TREATMENTS

Manual lymph drainage (MLD) can be performed on the body, neck, or face, and stimulates flow of lymph fluid through the lymphatic vessels from a swollen area to one that is working normally. Cell waste, water, and congestion can become trapped in the lymphatic vessels, resulting in swelling, known as edema. Massaging the swollen lymph area promotes movement of fluids, leading to a decrease in swelling. In addition, massaging areas that are not swollen creates space for fluid to flow to. MLD is often performed before and after surgery, as it helps to speed healing and cell metabolism. MLD is regularly used in facial massage, as the head and neck region contains over 300 lymph nodes. MLD can be performed manually or using an advanced machine where allowed. Some clients may incorporate manual lymph drainage into their home beauty routine through massage by hand or use of a tool such as a gua sha.

Spa body treatments are those intended for use on the whole body. Body wraps, scrubs, masks, and hydrotherapy fall under this umbrella.

- **Body wraps**: A product is applied to the body, then covered or wrapped in a linen or plastic sheet. These treatments may be used to hydrate, stimulate, detoxify, or remineralize the skin.
- **Body scrubs**: Exfoliating products, such as those containing ground nuts or seeds, salt, or sugar, are applied to the body and rubbed to scrub off dead skin cells. This leads to a brighter, more even appearing skin tone. These treatments are also referred to as polishes or glows and are often used to prepare the skin to receive additional treatments.
- **Body masks**: A clay, mud, or seaweed-based treatment is applied to the body to detoxify and remineralize. These may be used on their own or as the basis for a body wrap.
- **Hydrotherapy**: Any treatment that uses water as liquid, ice, or steam. The benefits vary widely and are dependent upon the treatment. Saunas, cold plunges, steam rooms, and hot tubs are all examples.

Some techniques to relax the body that may be used in spas are not yet considered mainstream. These are referred to as alternative relaxation treatments.

- **Balneotherapy**: The use of water baths containing salts and minerals, muds, enzymes or peat to treat physical ailments.
- **Stone massage**: The use of hot or cold stones in massage.
- **Foot reflexology**: A massage technique that applies pressure to a zone of the foot that corresponds to an area of the body.

- **Ayurveda**: An ancient Indian medical system that classifies the mind and body into one of three types based on one's physical characteristics. An individual's "type" determines their ideal lifestyle.
- **Endermologie**: A vacuum massage treatment that reduces cellulite and tightens skin. It stimulates the lymphatic system, breaks up fat, and reduces fluid retention.
- **Reiki**: A Japanese stress relief technique in which an unseen energy in the body is rearranged by the movement of hands around the body.
- **Balancing chakras**: Ancient Hindu philosophy states that the human body has seven different vortexes through which energy is processed. These can become blocked or imbalanced and require realignment through a variety of processes.

Cellulite is the bumpy or dimpled appearance in fatty areas, particularly the buttocks and thighs, caused by genetics and female hormones. The appearance is created by both swelling in dermal fat cells in combination with their proximity to the surface of the skin. A weakened or dehydrated epidermis makes cellulite appear more prominent; however, increasing hydration does not treat cellulite. Repairing cell and skin tissue damage is the key aspect to improving the appearance of cellulite which requires integrating a variety of nutrients and ingredients into a skincare routine. Ingredients such as B vitamins, amino acids, fatty acids, antioxidants, and anti-inflammatories are important for treatment of cellulite. It is important to note that many cellulite treatments are controversial and ineffective, such as detox diets, liposuction, and muscle stimulation systems. Other treatments such as manual lymph drainage, dermal fillers, laser treatments, and chemical peels only temporarily reduce the appearance of cellulite. To see long term results, treatments should be regularly performed by a professional.

Because sun exposure leads to skin cancer and premature signs of aging, it is important that estheticians advise their client to avoid unprotected exposure. Sunless tanning is a safer alternative to tanning in the sun. Many salons offer sunless tanning in the form of a spray tan using either a booth with sprayers or a handheld spray gun. Dihydroxyacetone is applied to the skin, inducing a chemical process that causes skin cells to darken. However, dihydroxyacetone is colorless. As such, many tanning solutions come tinted with what is called a guide color so that it can be seen when applied. This prevents both overapplication and missed areas. Clients with respiratory issues should avoid spray tanning. Spray tans should not be applied to broken, dry, irritated, or recently tattooed or pierced skin. The results of a spray tan typically last seven to ten days. Some clients may wish to extend their tans through use of at home sunless tanners. These use the same chemicals as commercial spray tans and come in foam, lotion, and liquid forms.

EYELASH AND EYEBROW SERVICES

Artificial lashes are adhered to the natural lash line to create the appearance of length and fullness. They are made from human, animal, or synthetic hair and are available in a variety of natural and unnatural colors. The three common types of lashes are band, tab, and individual. Band lashes are artificial lashes on a strip meant to be adhered across the lash line. They are also referred to as strip lashes. Tabs are clusters of three to four lashes adhered in intervals on the lash line. Individual lashes are applied one at a time as desired on the lash line. Eyelash adhesive, a glue formulated for use around the eyes, is used to hold the lashes in place. Artificial lashes should not be used on clients experiencing any kind of irritation on, in, or around the eyes, or with medical conditions such as pregnancy, glaucoma, or asthma, or on individuals receiving chemotherapy. Lashes may be removed by softening the adhesive with a makeup remover or warm cloth, then gently pulling to remove.

Lash tinting, extensions, and perming are all examples of services performed on natural eyelashes.

- **Lash tinting**: Typically used on clients with light lashes, a tint that will last for several weeks is applied to the lashes to darken them. Lash tinting may also be performed on the brows. A lash and brow safe hair dye is applied, allowed to sit per the manufacturer's instructions, then removed. This gives clients the appearance of fuller lashes and brows without having to fill them in daily using other cosmetic methods.
- **Lash extensions**: Synthetic or natural hairs are applied to client's individual lashes using a long-lasting adhesive. They remain on the lashes for up to two months. This gives clients the look of longer and fuller lashes without the need to wear mascara or apply artificial lashes daily.
- **Lash perming**: This process chemically curls the eye lashes, similar to perms that are applied to the hair. Perming is typically used on full, dark lashes to provide them with shape to create a desired look without the need to apply mascara daily.

Creating the ideal eyebrow shapes starts with mapping the brows. When an esthetician maps a client's brows, they will need a straightedge and a brow pencil. First, the straightedge is used to trace a vertical line from the outer corner of the nose to the inner corner of the eye and upward to the brow bone. This is where the brow should begin. Another line is traced from the outer corner of the nose to the outer corner of the eye and outward to the brow bone. This is where the brow should end. A third and final line is traced from the outside of the iris to the brow bone. This line indicates where the arch, or highest part of the brow, should be. Hair beyond these points should be removed and areas where hair is sparse should be filled in. While this process is considered a best practice when shaping brows, it may be necessary to modify this process for some clients based on their face shape. Brows with a high arch make round faces appear more narrow and square faces appear more oval, while lowering the arch can make long faces appear shorter.

HAIR REMOVAL METHODS AND PROCEDURES

Depilation is a form of temporary hair removal that removes hair at or near skin level. Shaving and use of chemical depilatories are the most common examples. In contrast to epilation, the process of removing hair from the bottom of the follicle, depilation is usually quicker, cheaper, and pain free. Because the hair is removed at the surface of the skin, the effects of depilation do not last as long as epilation treatments and must be performed more often. Depilation is typically performed by clients at home.

- **Shaving**: Uses a razor to remove hair at the skin's surface. Typically performed on the legs and underarms for female clients and the face for male clients. Hair typically grows back within one to four days and is rough, also known as stubble.
- **Chemical depilatory**: Chemical substances used to dissolve hairs on the skin's surface. Typically used on the face, legs, or underarms. Regrowth is slower and softer than shaving. However, the chemicals used can produce a strong, unpleasant odor and may irritate the skin if not used properly.

Epilation is the removal of hair from the bottom of the follicle. Hair that has been removed using epilation methods takes longer to grow back than hair that was removed by depilation. Epilation is more painful than depilation.

- **Tweezing**: Uses tweezers to remove hairs one at a time. Most often used in the eyebrow area to remove stray hairs.
- **Threading**: Also known as banding. Uses a looped cotton thread to glide over and pull out hairs. Most commonly used on the eyebrows and upper lip.
- **Waxing**: A heated wax, typically made of resins and beeswax, is applied to the skin and then removed. Soft wax requires a cloth strip to be laid across the wax before it hardens. Pulling the strip is what removes the hair. Hard wax can be removed by hand.
- **Sugaring**: Similar to waxing, but performed using a sugar-based paste that is spread on the skin, then pulled in the direction of hair growth. Commonly performed by estheticians on the legs, arms, back, or other large patches of hair growth.

Soft wax is made of rosins, which are resins that adhere to the skin. Soft wax has a honey-like consistency that must be heated before applying to the skin. **Hard wax** is also made of rosins with added wax, such as candelilla or carnauba, but comes in a brick, bead, or pellet format that must be melted to a smooth consistency before applying to the skin. Another difference between soft and hard wax is that soft wax requires a fabric strip to be placed over the wax for removal, whereas hard wax is removed by lifting the edge of hardened wax and pulling. All waxing should be preceded by cleansing the area. Soft wax requires application of a product such as witch hazel or tea tree oil to the area followed by application of baby powder. Both methods of waxing require post treatment with oil or lotion to soothe the skin. Soft wax is typically used on larger areas of the body such as the back and legs, while hard wax is used in smaller areas such as the brows and bikini area. However, the esthetician may choose which wax they prefer based on the needs of their client.

All eyebrow waxing processes begin by placing protective paper under the client, protecting the client's hair, and cleansing the area to be waxed. The esthetician will then position the brows into the agreed upon shape established in the consultation, or they will map out the brows and gain client approval before beginning hair removal. When using hard wax, an applicator is dipped into the wax and scraped on the underside of the warmer to remove any excess wax. The esthetician will stand behind the client and apply wax under the brow against the direction of hair growth, then again in the direction of hair growth. This may be done two to three times to cover the hair. When the wax hardens and is opaque, the esthetician will lift the edge and grasp it with their thumb and forefinger. Holding the skin taut, they will quickly pull against the direction of hair growth to remove the wax, then use their hand to apply pressure to the waxed area. This is repeated on the upper side of the brow, then on the second eyebrow.

Once protective paper has been placed under the client and their hair has been protected, the esthetician will cleanse the area to be waxed. Using the shape agreed upon in the consultation or the shape drawn during eyebrow mapping as a guide, the esthetician will pretreat the skin with either a pre wax treatment from the manufacturer of the wax or with a thin layer of tea tree oil followed by baby powder. An applicator is dipped into the wax and scraped against the warmer to remove the excess wax. The esthetician will stand behind the client and glide the wax along the underside of the brow at a 45-degree angle in the direction of hair growth. A cloth strip is placed over the wax and rubbed onto the area. The esthetician will use their dominant hand to grip the cloth while using their nondominant hand to pull the skin taut. The cloth is then quickly removed, and this process is then repeated above the brow and on the second brow.

The underarm, also referred to as the axilla, can be more complex to wax than other areas, as the hair grows in several different directions and converges in the middle. Hard wax is the optimal choice for this area. The underarm should be waxed in sections from the outer edges toward the center. A soothing lotion should be applied to each section after waxing.

Selecting which wax to use on the arms and hands depends on the nature of the hair. If hair is strong and unruly, it is best to use soft wax. While it will take longer, hard wax produces better results on soft hair or hair that has never been removed. Arms are waxed beginning with the inner arm before moving to the outer arm, followed by the upper arm if desired. For hands, hair is removed from the back of the hand first, then the knuckle. Aftercare lotion should be applied at the conclusion of waxing.

Upper body waxing may be performed on female or male clients, but their needs may differ, so it is important for the esthetician to perform a thorough consultation before beginning. Draping the client and cleansing the skin is necessary during all upper body wax treatments. On female clients, hair should be waxed from the outer edge of the areola outward, extra care should be taken to avoid contact with the areolas. For male clients, it may be necessary to trim the hair to a more manageable length before waxing. Wax should be applied first to the furthest, lower outer edge of the chest and then worked inward. Once the outer edge of hair on the furthest side has been removed, this will be repeated on the nearest side. The hair in the center is removed last. Some clients may want to have the hair from their back removed. Similar to chest hair, back hair can be trimmed before waxing to make it more manageable. The esthetician will begin waxing at the bottom outer edge of the torso and work upwards and repeat on the other side. The spine is then waxed followed by the shoulders. Aftercare lotion should be applied after all waxing treatments.

Lower body waxing includes the bikini area and legs and either hard or soft waxes can be used. The area to be waxed should be cleansed and prepped according to the manufacturer instructions of the wax. Bikini waxes fall under one of three styles, American or Standard, French, or Brazilian. The esthetician should confirm with the client what style they desire. Hair longer than half an inch should be trimmed so that it is more manageable before waxing. Wax is applied and removed from the outer edges inward until the desired style is achieved. Leg waxing starts with the tops of the feet and toes before moving to the inside ankle and then working outward until the front of the lower leg is fully waxed. This is followed by waxing the knee. The front side of the upper leg is then waxed and followed by the back of the leg. The client will then roll onto their stomachs for the removal of the back side of the lower leg hair.

Permanent hair removal and reduction may be achieved through electrolysis, laser hair removal, or intense pulsed light. In **electrolysis**, a thin probe is inserted into the hair follicle where the root is destroyed by either an electrical current, **thermolysis**, or a chemical reaction called **galvanic electrolysis**. Because it is effective on all skin and hair types, electrolysis is the only form of permanent hair removal approved by the FDA and AMA. It is ideal for areas like eyebrows where hair removal should be precise. Extensive electrolysis may take months or years to complete on larger areas and is often found to be painful. Laser and intense pulsed light (IPL) are forms of permanent hair reduction, meaning they reduce the amount of hair but do not remove it completely. **Laser** treatments heat up the pigment in the hair and damage the follicles to delay further growth. This treatment is ideal for candidates with darker hair. **IPL** uses pulses of light to make the hair enter its resting phase, then fall out.

Hair on the upper lip grows downward and out following the natural curve of the lip. If using a hard wax, all of the hair may be removed with one application. Using a soft wax requires hair to be removed on one side before moving to the other. Because the hair around the lip grows so close to the vermillion border, the border of the lips, special care should be taken to avoid getting wax on the lips as they are too sensitive and fragile to withstand forced removal of wax.

A chin wax refers to waxing both the chin and jaw. This should not be the first choice of hair removal in this area as tweezing is usually sufficient. If a client requests waxing, the throat and jawline are waxed first, followed by the chin. Similar to chin waxing, waxing should not be the primary hair removal method for the side of the face. If the area must be waxed, hard wax should be applied and removed in the direction of hair growth. All areas to be waxed should be cleansed before beginning and treated with a lotion or oil after completion.

WELLNESS PROGRAMS

Wellness programs are designed to enhance an individual's overall well-being. Common examples of wellness treatments in salons and spas include massages and spa treatments such as body wraps, body scrubs, and mud baths. Some salons and spas may have saunas, steam rooms, whirlpools, and jet baths clients can access. Medical spas are able to provide treatments like vitamin injections and light treatments. Any treatment can be considered a step toward wellness if it makes the client feel as though they are improving their overall health. Estheticians may offer a loyalty or pre-purchase program to earn free or discounted treatments for wellness treatments that will be performed frequently. Typically, this will occur after paying for a certain number of treatments or after purchasing a set number of services to be used over time. Some wellness treatments require recurring and increasingly potent procedures. These are commonly marketed and implemented as a program to ensure a client stays on track with treatment.

Esthetician Practice Test

Want to take this practice test in an online interactive format?
Check out the bonus page, which includes interactive practice questions and much more:
mometrix.com/bonus948/esthetician

1. According to NIC Infection Control and Safety Standards, which of the following is a standard procedure if a blood spill should occur?

    a. Bag all blood- contaminated articles.
    b. Documenting the incident in the blood spill log.
    c. Apply a liquid styptic container to the injury.
    d. Store all disinfected implements in a covered container.

2. Which of the following do streptococci bring about?

    a. Syphilis
    b. HIV
    c. Blood poisoning
    d. Comedones

3. Blood-borne pathogens are...

    a. Infectious microorganisms.
    b. Diplococcic.
    c. Parasites.
    d. Anthrax bacteria.

4. Mitosis can best be defined by which of the following statements?

    a. It is a process in which the number of chromosomes is reduced by half.
    b. It is a process during which molecules break down into smaller units, releasing energy.
    c. It is a process of cell duplication, where one cell forms two new cells that are genetically identical.
    d. It is a process by which the cells are nourished.

5. What is one of the principal functions of the skeletal system?

    a. It protects dendrites.
    b. It produces calcium.
    c. It aids in the metabolic process.
    d. It produces white and red blood cells.

6. Standards for EPA-registered disinfecting soak solutions dictate they should be changed...

    a. Once a week.
    b. Twice a day.
    c. Once a day.
    d. Every other day.

7. When people age, what happens to their subcutaneous tissue?

    a. It decreases.
    b. Adipose increases.
    c. It becomes dried out.
    d. It becomes pliant.

8. What is the effect of nicotine on the skin?

    a. It causes capillary walls to contract.
    b. It causes a narrowing of the blood vessels.
    c. It causes a rash on the skin.
    d. It causes dead cells to pile up.

9. Which of the following substances do the sebaceous glands utilize to lubricate the skin?

    a. Uric acid
    b. Ascorbic acid
    c. Lipids
    d. Lymph

10. In order to maintain healthy skin, a person should...

    a. Exercise twice a week.
    b. Pay attention to diet and water consumption.
    c. Have facials regularly.
    d. Use a moisturizer daily.

11. Why is it important for an esthetician to detect skin disorders and diseases in clients?

    a. The esthetician can then treat any existing skin disorders or diseases.
    b. The esthetician can then know to take special care when treating an infectious situation.
    c. The esthetician can then recognize which disorders or diseases need to be referred to a medical doctor.
    d. The esthetician can research the skin disease or disorder on the Internet.

12. Which of the following determines if a product is classified as a drug or a cosmetic?

a. OSHA
b. EPA
c. FAA
d. FDA

13. Quats, or quaternary ammonium compounds, are used by estheticians because...

a. They kill bacterial spores.
b. They disinfect tools quickly.
c. They don't soften plastic bottles.
d. They are odorless.

14. Which of the following is an accurate definition of pH?

a. It represents a mixture of two or more compounds.
b. It is known for its antiseptic properties.
c. It is used to treat infection.
d. It is the state of alkalinity or acidity of a given substance.

15. The Centers for Disease Control (CDC) recommends that estheticians should...

a. Insist that clients be warned about blood-borne pathogens.
b. Treat the blood of any client as if it were infected.
c. Ask clients for documentation as to their HIV status.
d. Always wash their hands before proceeding with a client.

16. Which of the following is a disorder of the sudoriferous glands?

a. Psoriasis
b. Eczema
c. Prickly heat
d. Cold sores

17. What are actinic keratoses?

a. Rough skin patches
b. Atopic dermatitis
c. Hives
d. Shingles

18. Milia are formed when...

a. A scar develops on the chest or back.
b. A macule grows on the surface of the skin.
c. Keratin forms beneath the outer layer of skin.
d. Inflamed skin swells.

19. Continuing cell division occurs in which of the following skin layers?

a. Hypodermis
b. Melanocyte
c. Keratin
d. Stratum basale

20. The atrium can best be described as...

a. One of four chambers of the human heart.
b. One of two ventricles.
c. A red corpuscle.
d. The superior labial.

21. Which of the following is an external factor affecting the skin?

a. Albinism
b. Collagen
c. Air conditioning
d. Vitiligo

22. A steatoma is...

a. A fatty deposit within a sebaceous gland.
b. A lesion due to excess oil.
c. A herpes outbreak.
d. An allergic reaction.

23. The purpose of a paraffin mask is...

a. To apply antioxidants.
b. To create a seal.
c. To help with oily skin.
d. To achieve a peel.

24. Which of the following best describes an enzyme?

a. It is the main source of energy.
b. It is a fibrous protein.
c. It is an essential fatty acid.
d. It acts as a catalyst.

25. According to OSHA's Bloodborne Pathogen Standard, employers must...

a. Regulate toxic substances.
b. Make Hepatitis B vaccinations available.
c. Use an EPA-registered disinfectant.
d. Follow ANSI standards for the safe use of lasers.

26. **Cellular recession can best be described as...**
    a. Producing pigment granules.
    b. A factor of intrinsic skin care.
    c. Nerve stimulation.
    d. Slowing down water evaporation.

27. **During the catagen stage of hair growth, the hair...**
    a. Goes into a resting phase.
    b. There is no hair growth at all.
    c. The outer root sheath shrinks.
    d. Cells in the root are dividing.

28. **Which of the following best describes an emulsion?**
    a. A substance with a pH below 7.0
    b. A synthetic surfactant
    c. A mix of immiscible substances
    d. A substance with solid particles evenly distributed.

29. **Sudoriferous glands are exocrine glands located in the...**
    a. Pores.
    b. Dermis.
    c. Apocrine glands.
    d. Capillaries.

30. **Which of the following is a function of the flexor muscle?**
    a. It moves the arms.
    b. It activates the buccal nerve.
    c. It connects two or more bones.
    d. It bends the knee.

31. **Tapotement is useful for what kind of skin condition?**
    a. Skin with acne
    b. Skin that is oily
    c. Sensitive skin
    d. Slack skin

32. **Skin that presents redness is...**
    a. Type VI skin.
    b. Sensitive skin.
    c. Combination skin.
    d. Dry skin.

33. An individual with a Fitzpatrick Scale classification of type IV is...

a. Free of blemishes.
b. Able to tan easily.
c. Hypopigmented.
d. Lacking in sebum production.

34. The Dr. Jacquet method is best described by which of the following?

a. Uses essential oils
b. Circular motion
c. Gentle twisting and kneading
d. Used on the scalp

35. Which of the following best describes what exfoliation does?

a. Reveals younger cells
b. Opens pores
c. Hydrates skin
d. Tones down redness

36. Hirsutism is defined as...

a. Increased circulation.
b. Raised lesions.
c. Excess hair.
d. Rough cells.

37. What does phytocosmetic mean?

a. Clean skin
b. A preservative
c. Type of massage
d. Of vegetable origin

38. During a client's first appointment, an esthetician should...

a. Test a new product.
b. Obtain a complete profile.
c. Discourage high expectations.
d. Determine if client has medical insurance.

39. Applying pressure to specific areas of the feet, hands and ears is called...

a. Shiatsu.
b. Petrissage.
c. Reflexology.
d. Grounding.

40. What is a humectant?

    a. The most popular botanical in cosmetics.

    b. An anti-bacterial agent.

    c. A product that removes residue of cleansers.

    d. A substance that furthers moisture retention.

41. Beta-glucan cream is known to…

    a. Activate macrophages.

    b. Remove dead cells.

    c. Transfer antioxidants.

    d. Trap moisture.

42. A treatment room checklist is important because…

    a. It impresses clients.

    b. It is required by state law.

    c. It helps the esthetician remember.

    d. It encourages sanitation.

43. What is the correct way to apply and remove facial products?

    a. Tap gently with finger tips.

    b. Use hot water to clean first.

    c. Stretch the skin for maximum effect.

    d. Use pressure so product will penetrate.

44. Which of the following is the correct order of applying makeup?

    a. Moisturizer, eyes, foundation, lips

    b. Foundation, moisturizer, eyes, lips

    c. Moisturizer, foundation, eyes, lips

    d. Foundation, eyes, lips, moisturizer

45. Iontophoresis is a process in which…

    a. A substance is separated into negative and positive ions.

    b. An electrode stimulation increases elastin production.

    c. A chemical reaction transforms sebum.

    d. A current is used for hair removal.

46. What is one of the benefits of vibration massage?

    a. It stimulates deep tissue layers.

    b. It helps alleviate pain.

    c. It stimulates glandular activity.

    d. It relieves headaches.

47. An individual with oily skin should use…

    a. A clay mask.
    b. A firming mask.
    c. A peel mask.
    d. A moisture mask.

48. The practice of electrical epilation is known as…

    a. Pulsed light.
    b. Electrolysis.
    c. Thermolysis.
    d. Electrology.

49. Which of the following is a good practice to avoid any contraindication issues with a client?

    a. Discontinue consultation with a client who has high blood pressure.
    b. Always keep work area clean and well organized.
    c. Have record cards with pre-printed questions.
    d. Make sure the temperature of the salon is comfortable.

50. When using essential oils in aromatherapy, an important rule of thumb is…

    a. To dilute with carrier oil.
    b. To avoid using candle diffusers.
    c. To avoid using in inhalation therapy.
    d. To not use oils with extenders.

Answer Key and Explanations

1. B: After treatment, the incident must be documented in the blood spill log. All blood-contaminated articles must be double bagged and labeled with red or orange biohazard warnings. A liquid styptic container should be used only with an applicator. Storing implements that have been disinfected is a dry storage standard and does not apply to a blood spill occurrence.

2. C: Streptococci cause blood poisoning. Syphilis is caused by the spirilla bacteria. HIV is not caused by bacteria. Comedones, also known as blackheads, are brought about by excess oil from the sebaceous glands.

3. A: Blood-borne pathogens are infectious bacteria and viruses. Diplococci are round bacteria usually found in pairs. Parasites are organisms that live in other organisms called hosts from which they get nourishment. Anthrax is a bacterial disease from infected animals or from anthrax spores dispersed in biological warfare.

4. C: Mitosis is a process of cell duplication with the function of cellular reproduction. Choice A is the definition for meiosis, with the function of sexual reproduction. Choice B is the definition of catabolism, and choice D is the definition of metabolism.

5. D: White and red blood cells are produced in bone marrow which fills the interior cavities of bones. Dendrites are nerve cell fibers and not associated with the skeletal system. The skeletal system stores calcium, it doesn't produce it. The metabolic process is also not associated with the skeletal system, but the cell system.

6. C: Changing disinfecting soak solutions each day ensures optimum safety. Choices A and D are too infrequent and the solution would lose its efficacy. Twice a day is not necessary.

7. A: When people age, their subcutis layer decreases, which causes wrinkling. Aging does not cause an increase in adipose or fatty tissue. And the subcutis neither dries out nor becomes pliant as a person gets older.

8. B: Nicotine causes the outermost blood vessels to contract. This leads to decreased oxygen and nutrients for the skin, with the result that the skin will wrinkle prematurely. Capillary walls cannot contract. There is no evidence that nicotine causes a rash or dead cells to accumulate on the surface of the skin.

9. C: The sebaceous glands secrete lipids to lubricate the skin. The oily mixture of lipids is called sebum. Ascorbic acid or vitamin C can be used to rejuvenate skin topically. Water doesn't have any lubricating properties. Lymph is the fluid that circulates through the lymphatic system and has no connection to the skin.

Mⓥmetrix

10. B: An adequate intake of the correct foods to supply vitamins and antioxidants and plenty of hydration has been shown to help maintain healthy skin. There is no evidence that regular exercise promotes healthy skin. Having regular facials and using a moisturizer on a regular basis does help keep skin healthy, but not without adequate and healthy diet and water consumption.

11. C: A thorough knowledge of skin disorders and diseases and their symptoms means the client will benefit from being referred to a physician in a timely manner. Choice A is incorrect; an esthetician should never try to treat a medical condition. An esthetician should be aware of procedures concerning infectious situations, but again, should not attempt treatment. While the Internet does offer access to a vast amount of knowledge, it is not a substitute for referral to a trained physician.

12. D: The Food and Drug Administration (FDA) is responsible for classifying whether a product is a drug or a cosmetic. OSHA (Occupational Health and Safety Administration) issues guidelines to be followed by estheticians, such as dealing with blood-borne pathogens. The EPA (Environmental Protection Agency) regulates products used in sanitizing, disinfecting and sterilizing compounds. The FAA, or Federal Aviation Administration, obviously has no connection to estheticians.

13. B: Quats are popular because they disinfect quickly and efficiently. Choice A is not correct; quats do not kill bacterial spores. Choices C and D are also incorrect; quats will soften the plastic in bottles and they are not odorless when used.

14. D: The degree of acidity or alkalinity is shown by the substance's pH scale, which ranges from zero to 14. A substance with a pH of less than seven is acidic, greater than seven is alkaline, and seven is neutral. A compound is a combination of matter. One substance known for its antiseptic properties would be hydrogen peroxide. An antibiotic is an example of something that could be used to treat an infection.

15. B: The CDC recommends that all blood and bodily fluids encountered in a salon be considered infected and be disposed of accordingly. Warning clients about blood-borne pathogens would not have any effect. Asking clients about their HIV status would not make sense from a business point of view. Washing one's hands is a common sense recommendation, and has nothing to do with CDC recommendations.

16. C: Prickly heat is an inflammation of the sudoriferous or sweat glands, brought on by exposure to excess heat. It causes a painful and burning itching sensation. Psoriasis is an inflammation of the skin. Eczema is a skin disease. Cold sores also occur on the skin and are caused by viral infection.

17. A: Actinic keratoses are pre-cancerous, rough patches of skin caused by exposure to the sun, usually seen in adults. Atopic dermatitis is a chronic skin disorder with itchy rashes found mostly in infants. Hives are red bumps caused by an allergic reaction. Shingles is a painful skin rash caused by the same virus that causes chicken pox.

Copyright © Mometrix Media. You have been licensed one copy of this document for personal use only. Any other reproduction or redistribution is strictly prohibited. All rights reserved. This content is provided for test preparation purposes only and does not imply an endorsement by Mometrix of any particular political, scientific, or religious point of view.

18. C: Milia are tiny cysts that appear when keratin forms below the outer layer of skin, creating tiny cysts. A keloid is a type of scar that develops on the chest, back or shoulders. Freckles occur when a macule, or discoloration of the skin, appears on the skin surface. When inflamed skin swells, pus-containing pustules or pimples form.

19. D: The stratum basale, or basal cell layer, is at the bottom of the epidermis. Cells are constantly dividing and being pushed up into the higher layers to replace dead cells. The hypodermis is the lowest layer of the integumentary system, composed of subcutaneous tissue which stores fat. Melanocyte is not a skin layer, but a specialized cell in the epidermis which produces the pigment melanin. Keratin is also not a layer of the skin, but a protein found in skin, hair and nails.

20. A: The atrium is one of four chambers that comprise the heart. Choice B is incorrect as there are also two ventricles and two atria in the heart. A red corpuscle is merely a red blood cell, responsible for delivering oxygen to body tissue. The superior labial comprise either the artery or vein that supply blood to the upper lip.

21. C: By lowering the relative humidity indoors, air conditioning can dehydrate the skin, causing wrinkles and lines. Albinism, the inability of the body to produce melanin, is genetically determined, and therefore not an external factor. Collagen, a fibrous protein found in the skin, occurs naturally. Vitiligo is a skin disorder where the body's production of melanin decreases, causing whitish spots to appear. Doctors do not yet know the cause.

22. A: A steatoma is a fatty deposit or a cyst in a sebaceous gland. Lesions due to excess oil occur in seborrhea. Herpes is a viral infection that causes cold sores, usually near the mouth. And choice D is not correct; a steatoma is not an allergic reaction.

23. B: The paraffin mask creates a vacuum-like seal, so the moisture drawn from the lower layers of skin mixes with the product being applied, providing a deep glow to the face. Antioxidants are usually applied topically during microdermabrasion. Paraffin masks do not help with oily skin. And exfoliation treatments usually include chemicals like alpha-hydroxy acids (AHAs).

24. D: An enzyme acts as a catalyst in the body, breaking down reactants into specific products. The main source of energy in the body is glucose, a simple sugar. Elastin is a fibrous protein; it is found in connective tissue. Omega-3 fatty acid is an essential fatty acid that cannot be produced in the body and is found in fish.

25. B: Employers must make available a Hepatitis B shot to any employee who could be exposed to blood. OSHA was established by Congress in 1970 to regulate toxic substances. The EPA (Environmental Protection Agency), not OSHA, is concerned with regulating disinfectants. ANSI (American National Standards Institute) has numerous voluntary standards, including one on the safe use of lasers. It is not affiliated with OSHA.

26. B: Cellular recession is an intrinsic factor in skin care, in that aging begins at the cellular level. When cell functions break down, cells don't perform activities that keep skin healthy, resulting in wrinkles and lines. Production of pigment granules is done by melanocytes. Nerve stimulation is accomplished through massage, which sends messages to the brain, lowering stress. Oil helps maintain water level in cells, slowing down water evaporation.

27. C: During the catagen stage, the outer root sheath shrinks and attaches to the hair's root. Hair goes into a resting phase during the telagen stage. Choice B is incorrect because at any given time a certain number of hairs will be in one of the three stages. Cells in the root of the hair are dividing in the anagen stage, the phase of active hair growth.

28. C: An emulsion is a combination of two or more immiscible (not blendable) substances joined together with an emulsifier. A substance with a pH below 7.0 is classified as an acid. A synthetic surfactant is a substance that, when dissolved in water, can remove dirt. A substance that has solid particles distributed in a liquid is called a suspension.

29. B: The sudoriferous (or sweat) glands are found in the second layer of skin, the dermis. The average person has over two million sweat glands. Pores on the skin's surface are connected to the sweat glands by tubes, apocrine glands are sweat glands found in the armpits and the genitals. Capillaries are blood vessels.

30. D: The flexor muscle is a skeletal muscle which, when contracted, bends a joint, like the knee or the wrist. Swinging or moving the arms is done through the trapezius muscle. The buccal nerve activates muscles in the mouth. Joints connect two or more bones.

31. D: Tapotement is a type of massage used for toning skin that is slack or sluggish. Choices A and C would contraindicate a massage. The Jacquet method is a massage used for oily skin conditions.

32 B: Redness is a sign of sensitive skin. Type VI skin is black skin. Combination skin can be seen when pores change from larger to medium outside the T-zone. Dry skin normally has small pores.

33. B: The Fitzpatrick Scale measures a person's tolerance to sunlight. Type IV individuals have a brown skin color, tan easily and rarely burn. None of the other choices concern sunlight. A person who is free of blemishes has normal skin. Hypopigmentation is characterized by white splotches on the skin. Someone who is lacking in sebum production would have dry skin.

34. C: The massage method developed by Dr. Jacquet uses a gentle twisting and kneading motion on the face to help clean out the oil ducts. Aromatherapy uses essential oils. A circular motion with the palms is effleurage. Friction massage is used on the scalp.

35. A: Exfoliation removes dead skin cells from the epidermis, revealing younger skin cells generated in the dermis. Warmth will open pores. Skin can be hydrated with moisturizers. And one way to tone down excessive redness is with a gel mask.

36. C: Hirsutism is defined as excess facial and body hair in women. The hair is usually dark and coarse. Increased circulation can be one of the benefits of a facial. Raised lesions or blemishes are called papules. Keratosis is a condition where rough cells appear on skin.

37. D: Phytocosmetic means of vegetable or plant origin, from the Greek word *phuton,* meaning "plant." Phytocosmetics have no synthetic ingredients. Clean skin is what estheticians strive to achieve. A phytocosmetic cannot be a type of massage or a preservative, as neither would make sense.

38. B: During the first appointment a complete profile should be completed, including the client's habits with regards to skin care. Testing a new product and asking if the client has medical insurance would not be ethical. And rather than discouraging a client from expecting too much, the esthetician should set reasonable goals.

39. C: Reflexology is a massage where pressure is applied to the feet, hands and ears to promote detoxification of the body. Shiatsu is Japanese for "finger pressure." It is believed it can help a person relax. Petrissage is a deep massage by kneading to help with circulation. Grounding is the process of having an electric current carried safely to the ground.

40. D: Humectants enhance the skin's ability to retain moisture, from the Latin word *humectus*, or "moist." Aloe is the most popular botanical used in the formulation of cosmetics. Green tea is known to be an anti-bacterial agent. And toners remove the residue left on the skin by cleansers.

41. A: Beta-glucan cream activates macrophages in connective tissue, which has been shown to maintain cell integrity and cause the skin to brighten and look younger. Exfoliators remove dead skin cells from the surface of the skin. Antioxidants are transferred by liposomes. Silicones help to hold moisture in the skin.

42. C: A treatment room checklist helps the esthetician remember all the details of setting up, cleaning and re-stocking products. It is not likely that a checklist would impress any clients, and it is not required by any laws or regulations. Choice D does not make any sense.

43. A: Tapping gently with fingers increases blood circulation and ensures the product will penetrate more deeply. Using hot water to clean dries out the skin; warm water is best. Stretching the skin or applying pressure will not achieve anything and might even hurt.

44. C: Hydration of the face makes the skin smooth. The other steps follow logically, concluding with applying lip color. The other choices are illogical in order, and therefore not correct.

45. B: Iontophoresis uses electrodes to send an electric current into the face, which stimulates elastin production while vitamins are added, resulting in a younger looking face. Ionization is defined as a substance breaking down into positive and negative ions. Saponification is a chemical reaction in which sebum is transformed. A process for hair removal is called thermolysis, which uses electric current to provide heat to the follicle.

46. B: Vibration massage can alleviate pain by sedating the nervous system through vibrating. Petrissage stimulates deep tissue layers. Friction massage stimulates glandular activity of the skin. Acupressure, which recognizes the same points as acupuncture, can alleviate headaches. It uses the hands instead of needles.

47. A: A clay mask will absorb excess oil, clean the skin and remove blackheads. A firming mask, meant for mature skin, increases the skin's moisture and reduces fine lines so the face looks younger. A peel mask will exfoliate the skin and add a glow to dull, lifeless skin. A moisture mask will help dry skin by sealing moisture in. When wiped off, a layer remains, and skin is softer.

48. D: Electrology is the procedure of using electrical epilation to remove hair. Pulsed light is a procedure of photorejuvenation, used to treat some skin conditions. Electrolysis is the actual removing of the hair. Thermolysis is one method of electrolysis where a radio transmitter produces heat that causes electrocoagulation of the hair follicle.

49. C: Contraindication issues can be avoided by having client record cards with pre-printed questions that can be checked off as answered and then signed by the client and dated. A client who says he or she has high blood pressure would merely have to provide a letter from a physician authorizing any procedures. Choices B and C are common sense precautions and have nothing to do with contraindications.

50. A: Essential oils are very concentrated and should not be applied directly. Always read the instructions on the bottle. Candle diffusers are fine; they provide a light fragrance and add ambience, but usually aren't strong enough to achieve therapeutic benefits. Inhalation of essential oils is also fine, either used with diffusers or compresses, but not for prolonged periods. And oils that have extenders are also fine. Many extenders are added to make the oil more pourable. Research what is used for the extender.

How to Overcome Test Anxiety

Just the thought of taking a test is enough to make most people a little nervous. A test is an important event that can have a long-term impact on your future, so it's important to take it seriously and it's natural to feel anxious about performing well. But just because anxiety is normal, that doesn't mean that it's helpful in test taking, or that you should simply accept it as part of your life. Anxiety can have a variety of effects. These effects can be mild, like making you feel slightly nervous, or severe, like blocking your ability to focus or remember even a simple detail.

If you experience test anxiety—whether severe or mild—it's important to know how to beat it. To discover this, first you need to understand what causes test anxiety.

Causes of Test Anxiety

While we often think of anxiety as an uncontrollable emotional state, it can actually be caused by simple, practical things. One of the most common causes of test anxiety is that a person does not feel adequately prepared for their test. This feeling can be the result of many different issues such as poor study habits or lack of organization, but the most common culprit is time management. Starting to study too late, failing to organize your study time to cover all of the material, or being distracted while you study will mean that you're not well prepared for the test. This may lead to cramming the night before, which will cause you to be physically and mentally exhausted for the test. Poor time management also contributes to feelings of stress, fear, and hopelessness as you realize you are not well prepared but don't know what to do about it.

Other times, test anxiety is not related to your preparation for the test but comes from unresolved fear. This may be a past failure on a test, or poor performance on tests in general. It may come from comparing yourself to others who seem to be performing better or from the stress of living up to expectations. Anxiety may be driven by fears of the future—how failure on this test would affect your educational and career goals. These fears are often completely irrational, but they can still negatively impact your test performance.

Elements of Test Anxiety

As mentioned earlier, test anxiety is considered to be an emotional state, but it has physical and mental components as well. Sometimes you may not even realize that you are suffering from test anxiety until you notice the physical symptoms. These can include trembling hands, rapid heartbeat, sweating, nausea, and tense muscles. Extreme anxiety may lead to fainting or vomiting. Obviously, any of these symptoms can have a negative impact on testing. It is important to recognize them as soon as they begin to occur so that you can address the problem before it damages your performance.

The mental components of test anxiety include trouble focusing and inability to remember learned information. During a test, your mind is on high alert, which can help you recall information and stay focused for an extended period of time. However, anxiety interferes with your mind's natural processes, causing you to blank out, even on the questions you know well. The strain of testing during anxiety makes it difficult to stay focused, especially on a test that may take several hours. Extreme anxiety can take a huge mental toll, making it difficult not only to recall test information but even to understand the test questions or pull your thoughts together.

Effects of Test Anxiety

Test anxiety is like a disease—if left untreated, it will get progressively worse. Anxiety leads to poor performance, and this reinforces the feelings of fear and failure, which in turn lead to poor performances on subsequent tests. It can grow from a mild nervousness to a crippling condition. If allowed to progress, test anxiety can have a big impact on your schooling, and consequently on your future.

Test anxiety can spread to other parts of your life. Anxiety on tests can become anxiety in any stressful situation, and blanking on a test can turn into panicking in a job situation. But fortunately, you don't have to let anxiety rule your testing and determine your grades. There are a number of relatively simple steps you can take to move past anxiety and function normally on a test and in the rest of life.

Physical Steps for Beating Test Anxiety

While test anxiety is a serious problem, the good news is that it can be overcome. It doesn't have to control your ability to think and remember information. While it may take time, you can begin taking steps today to beat anxiety.

Just as your first hint that you may be struggling with anxiety comes from the physical symptoms, the first step to treating it is also physical. Rest is crucial for having a clear, strong mind. If you are tired, it is much easier to give in to anxiety. But if you establish good sleep habits, your body and mind will be ready to perform optimally, without the strain of exhaustion. Additionally, sleeping well helps you to retain information better, so you're more likely to recall the answers when you see the test questions.

Getting good sleep means more than going to bed on time. It's important to allow your brain time to relax. Take study breaks from time to time so it doesn't get overworked, and don't study right before bed. Take time to rest your mind before trying to rest your body, or you may find it difficult to fall asleep.

Along with sleep, other aspects of physical health are important in preparing for a test. Good nutrition is vital for good brain function. Sugary foods and drinks may give a burst of energy but this burst is followed by a crash, both physically and emotionally. Instead, fuel your body with protein and vitamin-rich foods.

Also, drink plenty of water. Dehydration can lead to headaches and exhaustion, especially if your brain is already under stress from the rigors of the test. Particularly if your test is a long one, drink water during the breaks. And if possible, take an energy-boosting snack to eat between sections.

Along with sleep and diet, a third important part of physical health is exercise. Maintaining a steady workout schedule is helpful, but even taking 5-minute study breaks to walk can help get your blood pumping faster and clear your head. Exercise also releases endorphins, which contribute to a positive feeling and can help combat test anxiety.

When you nurture your physical health, you are also contributing to your mental health. If your body is healthy, your mind is much more likely to be healthy as well. So take time to rest, nourish your body with healthy food and water, and get moving as much as possible. Taking these physical steps will make you stronger and more able to take the mental steps necessary to overcome test anxiety.

Mental Steps for Beating Test Anxiety

Working on the mental side of test anxiety can be more challenging, but as with the physical side, there are clear steps you can take to overcome it. As mentioned earlier, test anxiety often stems from lack of preparation, so the obvious solution is to prepare for the test. Effective studying may be the most important weapon you have for beating test anxiety, but you can and should employ several other mental tools to combat fear.

First, boost your confidence by reminding yourself of past success—tests or projects that you aced. If you're putting as much effort into preparing for this test as you did for those, there's no reason you should expect to fail here. Work hard to prepare; then trust your preparation.

Second, surround yourself with encouraging people. It can be helpful to find a study group, but be sure that the people you're around will encourage a positive attitude. If you spend time with others who are anxious or cynical, this will only contribute to your own anxiety. Look for others who are motivated to study hard from a desire to succeed, not from a fear of failure.

Third, reward yourself. A test is physically and mentally tiring, even without anxiety, and it can be helpful to have something to look forward to. Plan an activity following the test, regardless of the outcome, such as going to a movie or getting ice cream.

When you are taking the test, if you find yourself beginning to feel anxious, remind yourself that you know the material. Visualize successfully completing the test. Then take a few deep, relaxing breaths and return to it. Work through the questions carefully but with confidence, knowing that you are capable of succeeding.

Developing a healthy mental approach to test taking will also aid in other areas of life. Test anxiety affects more than just the actual test—it can be damaging to your mental health and even contribute to depression. It's important to beat test anxiety before it becomes a problem for more than testing.

Study Strategy

Being prepared for the test is necessary to combat anxiety, but what does being prepared look like? You may study for hours on end and still not feel prepared. What you need is a strategy for test prep. The next few pages outline our recommended steps to help you plan out and conquer the challenge of preparation.

STEP 1: SCOPE OUT THE TEST

Learn everything you can about the format (multiple choice, essay, etc.) and what will be on the test. Gather any study materials, course outlines, or sample exams that may be available. Not only will this help you to prepare, but knowing what to expect can help to alleviate test anxiety.

STEP 2: MAP OUT THE MATERIAL

Look through the textbook or study guide and make note of how many chapters or sections it has. Then divide these over the time you have. For example, if a book has 15 chapters and you have five days to study, you need to cover three chapters each day. Even better, if you have the time, leave an extra day at the end for overall review after you have gone through the material in depth.

If time is limited, you may need to prioritize the material. Look through it and make note of which sections you think you already have a good grasp on, and which need review. While you are studying, skim quickly through the familiar sections and take more time on the challenging parts. Write out your plan so you don't get lost as you go. Having a written plan also helps you feel more in control of the study, so anxiety is less likely to arise from feeling overwhelmed at the amount to cover.

STEP 3: GATHER YOUR TOOLS

Decide what study method works best for you. Do you prefer to highlight in the book as you study and then go back over the highlighted portions? Or do you type out notes of the important information? Or is it helpful to make flashcards that you can carry with you? Assemble the pens, index cards, highlighters, post-it notes, and any other materials you may need so you won't be distracted by getting up to find things while you study.

If you're having a hard time retaining the information or organizing your notes, experiment with different methods. For example, try color-coding by subject with colored pens, highlighters, or post-it notes. If you learn better by hearing, try recording yourself reading your notes so you can listen while in the car, working out, or simply sitting at your desk. Ask a friend to quiz you from your flashcards, or try teaching someone the material to solidify it in your mind.

STEP 4: CREATE YOUR ENVIRONMENT

It's important to avoid distractions while you study. This includes both the obvious distractions like visitors and the subtle distractions like an uncomfortable chair (or a too-comfortable couch that makes you want to fall asleep). Set up the best study environment possible: good lighting and a comfortable work area. If background music helps you focus, you may want to turn it on, but otherwise keep the room quiet. If you are using a computer to take notes, be sure you don't have any other windows open, especially applications like social media, games, or anything else that could distract you. Silence your phone and turn off notifications. Be sure to keep water close by so you stay hydrated while you study (but avoid unhealthy drinks and snacks).

Also, take into account the best time of day to study. Are you freshest first thing in the morning? Try to set aside some time then to work through the material. Is your mind clearer in the afternoon or evening? Schedule your study session then. Another method is to study at the same time of day that you will take the test, so that your brain gets used to working on the material at that time and will be ready to focus at test time.

STEP 5: STUDY!

Once you have done all the study preparation, it's time to settle into the actual studying. Sit down, take a few moments to settle your mind so you can focus, and begin to follow your study plan. Don't give in to distractions or let yourself procrastinate. This is your time to prepare so you'll be ready to fearlessly approach the test. Make the most of the time and stay focused.

Of course, you don't want to burn out. If you study too long you may find that you're not retaining the information very well. Take regular study breaks. For example, taking five minutes out of every hour to walk briskly, breathing deeply and swinging your arms, can help your mind stay fresh.

As you get to the end of each chapter or section, it's a good idea to do a quick review. Remind yourself of what you learned and work on any difficult parts. When you feel that you've mastered the material, move on to the next part. At the end of your study session, briefly skim through your notes again.

But while review is helpful, cramming last minute is NOT. If at all possible, work ahead so that you won't need to fit all your study into the last day. Cramming overloads your brain with more information than it can process and retain, and your tired mind may struggle to recall even previously learned information when it is overwhelmed with last-minute study. Also, the urgent nature of cramming and the stress placed on your brain contribute to anxiety. You'll be more likely to go to the test feeling unprepared and having trouble thinking clearly.

So don't cram, and don't stay up late before the test, even just to review your notes at a leisurely pace. Your brain needs rest more than it needs to go over the information again. In fact, plan to finish your studies by noon or early afternoon the day before the test. Give your brain the rest of the day to relax or focus on other things, and get a good night's sleep. Then you will be fresh for the test and better able to recall what you've studied.

STEP 6: TAKE A PRACTICE TEST

Many courses offer sample tests, either online or in the study materials. This is an excellent resource to check whether you have mastered the material, as well as to prepare for the test format and environment.

Check the test format ahead of time: the number of questions, the type (multiple choice, free response, etc.), and the time limit. Then create a plan for working through them. For example, if you have 30 minutes to take a 60-question test, your limit is 30 seconds per question. Spend less time on the questions you know well so that you can take more time on the difficult ones.

If you have time to take several practice tests, take the first one open book, with no time limit. Work through the questions at your own pace and make sure you fully understand them. Gradually work up to taking a test under test conditions: sit at a desk with all study materials put away and set a timer. Pace yourself to make sure you finish the test with time to spare and go back to check your answers if you have time.

After each test, check your answers. On the questions you missed, be sure you understand why you missed them. Did you misread the question (tests can use tricky wording)? Did you forget the information? Or was it something you hadn't learned? Go back and study any shaky areas that the practice tests reveal.

Taking these tests not only helps with your grade, but also aids in combating test anxiety. If you're already used to the test conditions, you're less likely to worry about it, and working through tests until you're scoring well gives you a confidence boost. Go through the practice tests until you feel comfortable, and then you can go into the test knowing that you're ready for it.

Test Tips

On test day, you should be confident, knowing that you've prepared well and are ready to answer the questions. But aside from preparation, there are several test day strategies you can employ to maximize your performance.

First, as stated before, get a good night's sleep the night before the test (and for several nights before that, if possible). Go into the test with a fresh, alert mind rather than staying up late to study.

Try not to change too much about your normal routine on the day of the test. It's important to eat a nutritious breakfast, but if you normally don't eat breakfast at all, consider eating just a protein bar. If you're a coffee drinker, go ahead and have your normal coffee. Just make sure you time it so that the caffeine doesn't wear off right in the middle of your test. Avoid sugary beverages, and drink enough water to stay hydrated but not so much that you need a restroom break 10 minutes into the test. If your test isn't first thing in the morning, consider going for a walk or doing a light workout before the test to get your blood flowing.

Allow yourself enough time to get ready, and leave for the test with plenty of time to spare so you won't have the anxiety of scrambling to arrive in time. Another reason to be early is to select a good seat. It's helpful to sit away from doors and windows, which can be distracting. Find a good seat, get out your supplies, and settle your mind before the test begins.

When the test begins, start by going over the instructions carefully, even if you already know what to expect. Make sure you avoid any careless mistakes by following the directions.

Then begin working through the questions, pacing yourself as you've practiced. If you're not sure on an answer, don't spend too much time on it, and don't let it shake your confidence. Either skip it and come back later, or eliminate as many wrong answers as possible and guess among the remaining ones. Don't dwell on these questions as you continue—put them out of your mind and focus on what lies ahead.

Be sure to read all of the answer choices, even if you're sure the first one is the right answer. Sometimes you'll find a better one if you keep reading. But don't second-guess yourself if you do immediately know the answer. Your gut instinct is usually right. Don't let test anxiety rob you of the information you know.

If you have time at the end of the test (and if the test format allows), go back and review your answers. Be cautious about changing any, since your first instinct tends to be correct, but make sure you didn't misread any of the questions or accidentally mark the wrong answer choice. Look over any you skipped and make an educated guess.

At the end, leave the test feeling confident. You've done your best, so don't waste time worrying about your performance or wishing you could change anything. Instead, celebrate the successful completion of this test. And finally, use this test to learn how to deal with anxiety even better next time.

> **Review Video: Test Anxiety**
> Visit mometrix.com/academy and enter code: 100340

Important Qualification

Not all anxiety is created equal. If your test anxiety is causing major issues in your life beyond the classroom or testing center, or if you are experiencing troubling physical symptoms related to your anxiety, it may be a sign of a serious physiological or psychological condition. If this sounds like your situation, we strongly encourage you to seek professional help.

Additional Bonus Material

Due to our efforts to try to keep this book to a manageable length, we've created a link that will give you access to all of your additional bonus material:

mometrix.com/bonus948/esthetician